FEELING LIKE GOD

*A Spiritual Journey to
Emotional Wholeness*

David Crump

WIPF & STOCK · Eugene, Oregon

Wipf and Stock Publishers
199 W 8th Ave, Suite 3
Eugene, OR 97401

Feeling Like God
A Spiritual Journey to Emotional Wholeness
By and Crump, David M.
Copyright © 2006 by All rights reserved.
Softcover ISBN-13: 979-8-3852-0284-3
Hardcover ISBN-13: 979-8-3852-0285-0
eBook ISBN-13: 979-8-3852-0286-7
Publication date 9/19/2023
Previously published by Clements Publishing, 2006

This edition is a scanned facsimile of the original edition published in 2006.

CONTENTS

INTRODUCTION:
Confessions of a Young Atheist 7

1. WILL THE REAL GOD PLEASE STAND UP?
   Historical Backgrounds 15

2. IN THE SHADOW OF LOVE:
   Why Would God Be Angry? 43

3. DESIRE AND DISAPPOINTMENT:
   What Happens When God is Rejected? 69

4. GOD AS JEALOUS LOVER:
   Is Divine Pathos Pathological? 93

5. WHEN GOD GROWS TIRED:
   What Wears God Out? 117

6. SITUATIONS REAL AND IMAGINED:
   Are We Projecting Our Emotions onto God? 139

7. ETERNAL UNION:
   Learning to Feel Like God 165

8. A LONG AND WINDING ROAD:
   Sustaining Faith for the Journey 189

   NOTES 193

INTRODUCTION

CONFESSIONS OF A YOUNG ATHEIST

At the cynical age of thirteen I decided it was time to become an atheist. It was not a hasty decision made in the hormonal swamp of adolescent rebellion. I had been considering the ramifications of life with and without God since, at least, the age of ten, long before the whispers of teenage independence began their siren song. Even then I wondered how it was possible to honestly believe in something, someone, that had no beginning and no end. I remember lying on the top tier of the wooden-framed bunk bed I shared with my little brother, staring at the spackled ceiling only inches above my nose, pondering the imponderable. The "no end" part of God was never terribly problematic for me. I'm not sure why. I guess since modern medicine was regularly finding new ways to post-pone death, the idea of the cosmic "Great Physician" eluding death indefinitely was no great stretch.

My problem had always been with the "no beginning" part of God. How could I honestly believe in that? My inexperienced mind had tried to concoct any number of scenarios to explain the existence of a Being who not only would never die but had always been. I never lacked for a new idea, but I always failed to overcome the same, basic obstacle. In one way or another, each new late-night hypothesis was finally reduceable to just another version of a divine Big-Bang theory. And, of course, if God started with a bang, it did not matter how big that bang may have been, not only was it a beginning, it was a beginning born of something older than the resulting deity. Something had to set off the spark. So, in my earliest attempts at theological speculation, I found myself trying to figure out how the universe could have been created by a God with no beginning. Instead, I kept arriving back at a universe with no beginning giving birth to God. Yet, somehow I could not believe that this answer was right. So, with my racing mind finally slowed by exhaustion, I fell asleep each night praying that God would not be angry with doubters, not counting my failure to find answers against me. Finally, I would tentatively invite, and then reinvite, Jesus "to come into my heart" hoping that someone might be listening. I was never sure that my invitation had been heard much less accepted.

What eventually pushed me over the edge was not the mystery of God's nature but the clarity of God's demands. My youthful atheism was not so much the fruit of an intellectual decision as it was a moral one. Although I never did find satisfactory explanations to God's eternity, I had finally decided that God and I could live together with unanswered questions standing between us. After all, even at that tender age it had occurred to me that any God who could be thoroughly grasped by a twelve year old probably ought to be sitting in the desk next to mine working on penmanship.

My mind had moved on from ages ten to thirteen. The questions that kept me awake at night during the junior high school years concerned the personal challenges of God's moral expectations. I was especially uncomfortable with the order—given by the man I had been taught was God's son, Jesus—that I was expected to "love my neighbor as myself." This, to me, was unbearable. Fortunately, a complete transcript of my youthful, social pathologies is not necessary here. Let me simply say that, as an aspiring teenager who was becoming increasingly interested in living my own life, the idea of loving my fellow human beings did not rate very high on my priority list. God and I, it seemed, were developing irreconcilable differences. I was planning on a life that would allow me to leave the dregs of society—which was pretty much everyone but myself and my lastest crush—far, far behind. I was certain that I heard the hidden meadows of the Rocky Mountains and a career in wildlife biology calling my name.

So, the stage was set. It was only a matter of time. What I felt to be God's heavy-handed demands and my blossoming personality were becoming mutually exclusive. Furthermore, since my personality was plainly (at least, to my mind) God's own doing (I had never asked to be shy, insecure and painfully inept at making chit-chat), the resulting contradiction was God's fault. Here was another in a series of unanswered questions: Why would God have made me in such a way as to be constitutionally incapable of doing what I would eventually be asked to do? I could live with intellectual uncertainty, but hypocrisy was another kettle of fish. The most dreadful part of our family's weekly church attendance, apart from the endless droning of the shopping list labeled a congregational prayer, was watching the smiling adults, happy-faces firmly glued in place, making their customary rounds during the "fellowship hour." For all intents and purposes, most of these men and women were virtual strangers to one another. Unless you were a third-generation member of the founding fathers' in-crowd, few people ever saw the inside of another family's home. Yet, having fellowship meant pretending to care about each other—making promises of get-togethers which never took place; asking probing questions with a veneer of sympathy only to trundle off hastily the moment a tentative request for help seemed imminent. I knew from my fellow teenagers in the church youth group whose parents were sleeping in separate bedrooms; whose husband was cheating with whom; whose daughter would go all the way. As far as I could see, these people lived in two separate, discrete worlds. There was a Sunday world and a weekday world, and never the twain shall meet. Watching this scripted, religious dance was one thing; that was an ethnographical assignment I had learned to tolerate. Becoming another guilty player—smiling and pretending to love my neighbor when, in fact, I saw him as a pathetic game-player—was something I would not do.

In retrospect, I realize that I was judging quite ordinary people with a self-righteousness only a teenager could muster. But at the time, I was convinced that God was asking me to dine with the devil. I could not explain such a contradictory request, but I knew how I must respond to the invitation. God was boxing me into a corner, forcing me to choose between faithfulness to an invisible deity and faithfulness to my (very visible) self. What point was there in claiming to believe in God on Sundays while ignoring his daily directions? It was one thing to hear a Sunday School story about an old guy named Abraham who willingly stretched out his hand to slit his son's throat for God, it was quite another to be expected to do the same thing to myself. Since I was still not thoroughly convinced of God's existence anyway, but knew that I would have to face my own existence every day, I did the only thing I could. I opted for integrity. I told God goodbye.

However, God would not say goodbye to me. I held on to my atheism, quite privately, for about two years. Like so many others in the late 1960s, I superficially investigated different forms of eastern spirituality, reading parts of the *Bagavadgita*, and throwing myself whole-hog into the meditation that accompanied my passion for the martial arts. However, there was always an ebb and flow to my determination to remain an unbeliever. I suspect that the strength of my resolve was directly related to the shifting levels of my teenage angst. Yet, even when my personal confusion and anger at the world were most profound, I was continually haunted by one inescapable fact: in my heart-of-hearts I could not stop believing that Jesus of Nazareth had actually existed, was crucified and had risen from the dead. Don't ask me why I could never shake this conviction; I just couldn't. It stuck to me like a tar-baby. No matter how deeply I tried to bury it, it kept sticking out more and more stubbornly in my own mind. I would not call it a "faith" as much as it was a "pre-existing condition." Faith is something a person willingly embraces. This conviction, on the other hand, tracked me down relentlessly wherever I tried to hide, trapped me and showed no mercy. (Though now, in retrospect, I would say that I was shown nothing but mercy). As much as I wished I could cut the memory of Jesus out of my life, I found myself repeatedly attracted to his light like a stupid, helpless moth to the flame. And my memories of him burned, they burned deeply into my conscience. Call it parental brain-washing if you like. I am sure that many people would have labeled my lingering, religious consciousness the stubborn byproduct of environmental conditioning. I knew from first-hand experience how easy it was to explain away someone else's religious conviction by dropping that psychological boom every time a traditional, religious belief raised its head. There was just one problem. I could never sufficiently explain my own persistent, malingering belief. Or perhaps I should say that the explanation was never quite *satisfying*. However, that stubborn sense of dissatisfaction in the face of every logical explanation was about to be confronted with the most overwhelming sense of the presence of God.

Eventually, when I was sixteen I found myself alone on a church retreat, sitting in the backseat of a bus, reduced to tears by a voice inside my head. It was not an audible voice, but I heard it speak clearly enough to me: "You accuse others of hypocrisy, but you are a hypocrite yourself. Your unbelief is only an attempt to hide from a God you don't like. Your life is a game of hide-and-seek played between your mind and your heart, and one day soon I will show you how much you have to lose. Stop it now, and surrender."

That was it. I'm not joking. I heard those words (or something very close to them) in my head. Being clubbed with a baseball bat could not have felt more real to me at that moment. God had exploded from inside of me (the last place I thought to look!), escaping like a genie from a bottle, and now I was the one who had been enveloped, captured. I began a new journey that day. And I actually found myself uncomfortably relieved that my real-life charade was over. None of my intellectual or emotional questions had been resolved, but at least my spiritual schizophrenia could be laid to rest (only fitfully, however, as I would later discover). I now look back over some 30-odd years of life attempting to "walk" (as they say) with God. It has not been an easy journey. In the intervening decades I have regularly found myself facing a God I still do not always like or understand; at times I have even been tempted to walk away all over again. I periodically find myself facing a new day wondering, "What if life with God *is* just a fantasy after all?" On the other hand, there have also been those moments—all too occasional and fleeting, perhaps, but nonetheless real—when God's bright and shining presence has been the most, the only, "real" thing in my life. Through it all, I have always tried to remember one important lesson: If a God exists, then God is what God is, not what I might wish God to be. The supernatural is discovered in divine self-disclosure. I can only receive what God gives, try my best to understand that revelation and be amazed at what I cannot comprehend.

Such submission has raised many questions. But in this submission I have also found answers, answers which (believe it or not) have miraculously come to include wanting to love my neighbor as myself. What follows is an attempt to explain that transformation of mind and heart as the work of a Supreme Being whose decisions are not only the product of an infinite intellect, but also of an unfolding, divine emotional life.

The strategy for what follows is fairly straightforward. I will begin in chapter one by offering an historical overview surveying the longstanding debate about the feasibility of divine emotions, a very controversial subject throughout the history of western religious thought. Anticipating the landscape to be traversed in our journey may help us to avoid the pitfalls that I believe have caused others to stumble.

Chapters two through five will then explore the more controversial emotions, such as God's anger, desire, disappointment, jealousy and weariness. Can a perfect, eternal God actually experience emotions such as these? If so, what does that tell us about God? What do we mean when we say that God "feels"? Hopefully, we will discover that, while such passions may initially appear unbecoming to the divine character, they are actually the best demonstration that God is worth our time and attention.

Chapter six will attempt to unravel the personal dilemma of distinguishing God's emotions from our own emotional projections. How can I know that what I believe are God's feelings towards me are not actually my own feelings about myself; in which case, the knowledge of God is really nothing more than my own self-understanding? Is there a difference? If so, how do I learn to discriminate between the two?

Our final destination—union with God—is the subject of chapter seven. According to the Christian tradition, God has provided a way for our emotional healing as we are ultimately caught up into God's own perfected, emotional life. I will argue that the Christian tradition of the "incarnation" of Christ (the belief that God became human in Jesus of Nazareth), and its centrality to the ancient,

Christian teaching of "deification" (the idea that we may become like God) provide the answers we seek.

Finally, chapter eight will summarize our journey, from the exploration of God's own emotional life to its implications for our own emotional transformation, offering practical suggestions for how the reader may progress in his or her own quest for personal wholeness in relationship to God.

1

WILL THE REAL GOD PLEASE STAND UP?

Historical Backgrounds

What is Plato but Moses speaking Greek?
—Clement of Alexandria
Miscellanies, 1.22

*Oh, unhappy Aristotle!...
What indeed has Athens to do with Jerusalem?*
— Tertullian
Prescription Against Heretics, 7

The hyperventilating caller had left a shrill message on my office answering machine. Listening to his frayed voice, I could easily imagine blue veins rythmically bulging out the sides of his forehead: "You ought to be ashamed of yourself for teaching such trash! God does not have feelings. He is absolutely perfect and impenetrable. There is no point of contact, of any sort, between God and anything we would identify as human emotion!"

I had been a minister long enough to become well acquainted with irate parishioners, but I had never heard an outburst quite like this. The anonymous, male caller was nearly hysterical as he shouted into the phone. The final, resounding 'click' made it clear that he had thrown down the receiver in disgust.

The first attempt at an orthodox correction of my upcoming Sunday morning messages had been preserved for posterity on my AT&T voice-mail. My critic had not stopped to explain which church he represented, but he clearly believed that our congregation's advertisement headlining that month's series—*God Has Feelings, Too!*—was not only mistaken but dangerously corrupt.

Why? Why would anyone object to a description of God as a supreme being with emotions, personal qualities that have come to be called "the passions"? After all, doesn't the Bible define the Judaeo-Christian God as full of love? I John 4:8 goes so far as to say that "God is love." Isn't this same God also described in very personal terms as one who responds and interacts through his involvement in real, reciprocal relationships with people, becoming appropriately (and somewhat predictably) happy, saddened, disappointed and even jealous at various points in the Bible? The Old Testament book of Deuteronomy warns the people of Israel that if and when they abandon their God:

> Their idolatry will make the LORD jealous;
> (and) their evil will make God angry. *(*Deuteronomy 32:16)

In other words, the God of Moses responds emotionally to personal mistreatment.

In the New Testament, Jesus apparently held to the same personal, inter-active conception of his own God, telling his followers that when God's people fully embrace real relationship with heaven that:

> There is more rejoicing in heaven over one sinner who repents than over ninety-nine righteous people who do not need to repent! (Luke 15:7)

Heaven throws a party to celebrate anyone's genuine search for ultimate Truth, and God sits at the head of the table cutting the cake! What could be clearer?

WILL THE REAL GOD PLEASE STAND UP?

Actually, many things. As in so much of the god-talk that comes to be called theology, clarity is often in the eyes of the beholder. One person's crystaline image is another's muddy mess. God has a tendency to become one Rorschach ink blot among many, reflecting more about the viewer's unconscious preconceptions than God's own (possibly) divine reality. Even though my caller probably did not realize it, he was reflecting a long-standing theological tradition in the Christian church, both Roman Catholic and Protestant alike, which has claimed that the God of the universe is entirely free of anything we humans could recognize as passionate emotion. In fact, this tradition claims that passionlessness is an absolute necessity for anything hoping to lay claim to the authentic title of deity. For example, *The Westminster Confession of Faith*, composed by British clergymen in 1646 and still read by a variety of Presbyterian churchgoers today, offers the most commonly recited version of this belief. It says that God is "infinite in being and perfection, a most pure spirit, invisible, without body, parts, or passions..." (Chapter II, Article 1). Similarly, the *Thirty-Nine Articles* of the Anglican/Episcopal church says, "There is but one living and true God, everlasting, without body, parts, or passions..." (Article I).

Knowing all this, my caller's sentiments did not take me by surprise. I realized that his type were still around, even though I suspect that he represents a small minority of those who would claim to believe in God today, especially among Presbyterians and Episcopalians. My conversations with friends and neighbors suggests that, as we stumble into the early days of a new millenium, most people are wrestling with very different issues than my critic. If God is thought to exist at all—and this is the bigger question for most—then it is not difficult to imagine a deity somewhat like me—emotional, responsive, personal. Any God that hopes to stir up public interest today had best be personally significant, even emotionally intriguing. But to suggest any specific, personal portrait of the divine begs a prior question: Can *any* kind of personal God exist anywhere?

Our modern sense of religious uncertainty has not always been the norm in the Western world. In times past, God's existence would have been confidently assumed, and we would have been left to debate the subsequent questions of the deity's public nature and private idiosyncrasies. We could have asked such questions as: Does God have feelings? If so, can God's feelings towards me change? Against this historical background, my anonymous caller offers a helpful point of departure for our journey. Uncovering the historical roots of his protest will help to explain how we have come to a place in our contemporary world where thinking people usually have more doubts than certainties about anything we might call God. For the purposes of the present argument, I offer the suggestion that modern scepticism towards the traditional, Judaeo-Christian God is, in part, a predictable rebellion against two opposing solutions to the problem of divine passion.

CONSIDERING THE OPTIONS

Some have read the ancient, biblical stories with the faith of simple literalists. In other words, these believers have asserted that the biblical record ought to be taken at face value; it means what it says, quite literally, at each and every point.[1] Though to many this method is appealing in its simplicity, it may produce a terribly misshapen, unappealing picture of God. For example, reread the previous passage from the Old Testament book of Deuteronomy. How are we to respond to an angry God stirred to jealousy by our roving, religious eye? Or read Psalm 7:11,

> God is a righteous judge,
> a God who expresses wrath every day.

Here, it appears, is a description of God in a perpetual state of rage executing constant judgment and condemnation upon a continually failing human race. Elsewhere in the Old Testament, God is similarly portrayed as a thoroughly intimidating figure, subject to fits of jealousy, envy, vengence and periodic reversals of opinion as to whether he will wipe out humanity or let us live another day.

> The Lord was sorry to have ever made mankind on the earth;
> God's heart was filled with pain. So the Lord said, "I will wipe mankind from the face of the earth...". (Genesis 6:6-7)

WILL THE REAL GOD PLEASE STAND UP?

Since the Age of Enlightenment many have entertained this picture of God and christened it a *Deus horrendus* too frightening to seriously approach much less worship. A patently emotional, seemingly overly emotional, God of the Old Testament tradition, subject to petty whims and childish, uncontrollable outbursts, has been retired from serious consideration in this scientific era, and many would say that the absence is no great loss.

On the other hand, there has been another continuous line of devout believers in the Judaeo-Christian God who could also be called literalists in their way of reading the ancient stories. This tradition approaches the Old Testament text with equally sincere devotion. However, they have found a way to simultaneously accept the historical character of the Old Testament storyline, while rejecting the accompanying image of a frighteningly emotional God. The method is simple. They reject outright any and all descriptions of divine emotions. Their God cannot possess frightening emotions because God cannot possess any emotions, being safely ensconced above and beyond the petty and unpredictable morass of passion that plagues humanity.

Apparently, my anonymous protester had stood in this particular line of faith. Whether he knew it or not, he was defending an ancient method of describing God that extends at least as far back as the Greek philosophers. In fact, it is a portrait of the divine that has sometimes been dubbed the "God of the philosophers," a cosmic progeny born of the attempt to describe the God of the Hebrew prophets in the language of Greek metaphysics. However, as happens with the fruit of any such union, one couple's beautiful child is another's ugly pug; and so it has been with the traditional God of philosophical theology.

Many participants in this historical project of biblical and philosophical hybridization have called the results of their experiment "orthodoxy" (that is, the only acceptable way to think about and to describe God). Having managed to codify their particular vision of God by embedding their own outline into the historic Christian creeds and confessions, it has typically been this God of the philosophers who has been used as the standard for sifting the doctrinal wheat from the chaff. Thus as early as the fifth century

(A.D. 451), the bishops of the Council of Chalcedon decreed that anyone who dared to say that God experiences emotions—otherwise known as the passions—would be defrocked from the priesthood.[2]

However, while the guardians of this new orthodoxy staked their claim to being the only ones able to explain divine reality, others watching the birth of this passionless God were less enamored with the deity being offered to them. In fact, many would have hoped for a prompt miscarriage. From the earliest days there were fervent protests, especially from the originally Jewish wing of the Christian church. This loyal opposition party claimed that the use of Greek philosophical language was fundamentally incompatible with any faithful description of the God of the Bible.[3] If words are the vessels that carry meaning, they argued, then foreign words borrowed from pagan thinkers will inevitably leak the truths they cannot hold and distort the remainder however much or little it may be. This ancient debate over theological method (that is, how one ought to proceed in a discussion about the truth of God) not only drove a wedge between different schools of thought within the ancient church, but would eventually result in an ever-widening, intellectual chasm between historic Christianity and the rest of the Western world. The emotionless God of the philosophers had little appeal to Enlightenment thinkers. Once the emotional ties of family heritage and church tradition were replaced by the intellectual claims of enlightened, human reason, it took very little effort for "modern" men and women to cut themselves free from the old, religious confessions. It was a short step from the traditional, Christian God who had no "body, parts or passions" into an exploration of the growing crop of eighteenth- and nineteenth-century religious alternatives springing up in the new forms of deism, romanticism, transcendentalism and even atheism. In fact, it has been argued that the eventual rise of our modern religious uncertainties, and the rampant scepticism that attaches itself barnacle-like to any and all religious claims today, was the final fruit of a cultural and intellectual revolt against this very God of the philosophers.[4] Thus Ludwig Feuerbach, the father of modern, philosophical atheism whose views were largely popularized by Sigmund Freud (in psychology and psychoanalysis), Karl Marx (in politics and economics) and Friedrich Nietzsche (in philosophy and social theory), protests in his *Lectures on the Essence of Religion*:[5]

> How can an abstracted, nonsensuous, disembodied being, a being without sensuous needs, impulses, passion, expect me, a bodily, sensuous, real being, to emulate Him? . . . Man does not understand God, says theology, *but neither, says anthropology, does God understand men.* What does a God know of sensuous drives, needs, and passions?... ...Consequently, when a rationalist asks an atheist what atheism is, the proper answer is: Rationalism is a half-baked, incomplete atheism; atheism is complete and thoroughgoing rationalism.

I must confess that I find it equally difficult to be interested in this type of remote, dispassionate God. Any God so totally removed from my earthly experience of pain and pleasure as to be incapable of empathy should not be surprised if I eventually become as disinterested in heaven as heaven is seemingly oblivious to me. Let this abstracted, disembodied Being, without needs, impulses or passions, contemplate the divine navel, alone. When I need help, I would rather turn to a compassionate companion who knows about turmoil from first hand experience.

CONSTRUCTING THE IDEAL GOD

In order to understand why my telephone critic was so outraged, and perhaps why Feuerbach finally chose atheism over faith, we need to go back to the ancient Greeks, particularly Plato (427-347 B.C.) and his most influential pupil, Aristotle (384-322 B.C.). In book 7 of his work, *The Republic*, Plato tells a famous story of prisoners shackled to the floor inside a cave. With their backs to the mouth of the cave, all they are able to see are the flickering shadows cast by travelers outside, dancing ghost-like upon a cave wall ahead of them. Because they are chained, they cannot turn around to see the source of the shadows; they must simply make the most sensible associations possible between the shadow images they can see in front of them and the noisy hustle and bustle going on in the real world behind them. This is a description of the human predicament, according to Plato. The various objects we can see, touch and smell in this world are simply imperfect, temporary projections of the eternal Forms, or Ideals, found in the real world beyond. What we call a "chair" is only a chair because it shares in and reflects something of the eternally perfect form of "chairness." All that is beautiful and good in this world share these qualities because they somehow participate in the perfect Ideals of Beauty and Goodness found in eternity. We live in a shadow world. However, through the exercise of reason and the denial of physical desires, the discipline of philosophy can train the mind to move beyond these shifting shadows towards the proper contemplation of the eternal forms above.

Although Plato fine-tuned his view of the forms throughout his lifetime, the basic issues remain the same in his writings. This material world and the realm of the ideals are separate and distinct from each other. The visible world, the arena of the body and desire, is always changing; whereas the unseen forms, approached only through the mind, are constant.[6] To Greek thinking, perfection also meant unity or singleness, as opposed to the complexity of compound compositions (Plato was highly influenced in this regard by the the Greek mathematician, Pythagoras). Competing emotions meant complexity, the kind of complexity found only in the material world. Passion also often intruded itself, unsought and unwanted, into life. One's striving for recognition pulled against humility. Insecurity stood in the way of self-confident achievement. Love and anger often wrestled within the same heart. Such confusion was inherent to the emotions but would be completely out of place in the eternal world of ideals. Consequently, in his *Symposium* Plato states that the perfect form of beauty could only exist:

> ... with itself, by itself, in perfect *simplicity;* while all the beautiful things elsewhere partake of this beauty in such manner, that when they are born and perish it becomes neither less nor more and *nothing at all happens to it.*[7]

True beauty could never be subject to passion or the change inherent within it.

Towards the end of his career Plato wrote the work that would have the most profound influence upon the history of Judeao-Christian thought, the *Timaeus*.[8] Here was the first Greek account of divine creation. In this work, the eternal forms exist within the mind of God serving as the architectural pattern for the universe. The Creator is described as the (ultimate) Cause[9] and the Unmoved,[10] important terms to be taken up later by Aristotle in his own theology. God exists in the eternal world of being, while the creation exists in the temporal world of becoming. The world of being always is and never becomes; there is no change. The material world is always becoming and never is; there is only change. Again, these distinctions necessarily limit emotional experience to the created, material world of becoming. Passion effects change. Simply reflect upon the ambiguity inherent in our use of the word "moved." Whether we are moved (emotionally) by hearing Beethoven's 5th symphony or moved (physically) by the Mayflower trucking company, some sort of personal change has taken place, either internally or externally. This is precisely the sort of change that cannot occur in the Creator's realm of being, for change signifies becoming! Thus neither God nor the eternal forms can ever be subject to emotion. This clear-cut distinction between these two realms of existence causes the reader of the *Timaeus* to wonder whether the gulf between them is so large that the creator must forever remain unknowable. Plato's answer will become a favorite quotation among later Christian writers:

> To discover the maker and father of this universe is indeed a hard task, and having found him it would be impossible to tell everyone about him.[11]

Discovering the truth about God is too difficult for most and barely attainable for the devoted few. To the masses God must remain a mystery beyond description or apprehension. For everyone, including the philosopher, God may best be described in terms of what divinity is not. This sensible world of the perceptions is always changing. The creator, however, is beyond the senses, beyond perception and is unchanging. The deity is everything the world is not.[12] This Platonic observation on how to describe God, something that has come to be called the *via negationis* (the way of negation), will become an important tool for early Christian writers about God: *the clearest statements that anyone may make about God are denials.* Ultimately, God himself remains unknowable, even when he is the Father revealed through the Son, Jesus Christ.

True, in certain situations God may appear to undergo change, such as a change in disposition from rewarding the obedient to punishing the disobedient. But Plato explains this as a matter of appearances resulting from our changing circumstances not God's demeanor. God has not changed; we have. For example, when standing next to a growing adolescent an adult appears to grow shorter, but we know that it is the teenager not the parent who is actually changing height. Christian tradition will repeat similar analogies for centuries to come, most often in terms of a moving spectator watching an immovable pillar: if you walk around a pillar, it appears to move in its relationship to the surrounding structure; yet you know full well that the architecture is not moving, you are.[13] So it is with God and creation. Whenever God appears to change, we can be sure that it is actually some movement one way or another in our relationship to God that has changed. God does not change. We do.

Aristotle studied with Plato in the Athenian Academy for some 20 years, but he was far from being an ivory tower thinker. Not long after Plato's death he became tutor to Alexander, son of Philip of Macedon. This gave him a ringside seat to the court intrigue which eventually saw Alexander seated upon his father's throne and launched upon a military career that would see him conquer the known world and given the title Alexander the Great. However, once Alexander had risen to the throne (in 335 B.C.), rather than continue to follow his pupil across the globe, Aristotle returned to Athens and established his own school of philosophy at the Lyceum. His school of thought would become known for at least one major point of disagreement with his old teacher. Aristotle rejected Plato's theory of Forms. Plato himself had struggled to explain how the individual entities of this material world actually participate or share in the forms. In other words, exactly how *did* the forms impart something of their "formness" to the things dependent upon them in this world? The answer to that question was never clear.

Aristotle understood Plato's vagueness at this point to be a major flaw in his theory.[14] He believed that a clearer explanation of reality was available by exploring questions of causation, that is the process of cause-and-effect. What *caused* things to be what they were? How many different types of causation were there operating in the world, and how did they interact with one another? Of course, if one traces this process of cause-and-effect back far enough you will presumably reach a point of beginnings...or will you? Aristotle concluded that you must. There cannot be such a thing as infinite causation, so there must have been some original, eternal cause, the First Cause, the Unmoved Mover, what Aristotle called God.

Someone, or something, must have begun the cosmic ball rolling. But in order to be the first cause, it cannot have been caused or moved by anything else prior to itself. Thus it must cause without having been caused; it must move without having been moved. It must exist eternally without change.[15] Although this explanation of Aristotle's Unmoved Mover is somewhat simplified, it provides enough of the basic contours to show how his philosophy of God will eventually work quite nicely with Plato's theory of Forms to exclude emotion from the divine repertoire. On this both Plato and Aristotle firmly agree.

First, like Plato, Aristotle believed that emotion requires intrapersonal complexity and necessarily results in change, whereas the Unmoved Mover must be "without parts and indivisible."[16] If the First Cause was ever moved by emotion, it would exhibit a composite nature that was being influenced by something else prior to itself.

Second, Plato and Aristotle also agreed on the superiority of thinking over feeling. "Thinking is the most godlike of things in our experience."[17] Obviously, then, this is what God must spend eternity doing—thinking. Since God would only ponder the most worthy subjects, and since nothing is more worthy than God's own thinking, God must spend eternity thinking about divine thinking.[18] According to this view of God, emotion would only detract from that which reveals God's perfection.

Finally, Aristotle clarifies why change is incompatible in anything claiming perfection. "Any change would be a deterioration, and such a thing is already a kind of movement."[19] The Unmoved Mover cannot be moved, not even by Beethoven's 5th symphony. To change from one emotional state to another would mean that the First Cause either was or had been imperfect. Either it moved up the emotional scale, in which case it had previously been less than perfect; or it moved downwards, it which case it has slipped from perfection. In either event, emotion spells disaster for the divine.

CROSS-POLLINATING FROM THE GREEKS TO THE JEWS

Ideas travel. Powerful ideas travel far. If ethnic groups and their ways of explaining the world kept to themselves, history would be a simple matter of tabulating how different civilizations had kept to their own neck of the woods. But we all know that this is not the way the world works. Neither people nor their ideas have ever been very good at staying inside their original boundaries. Barriers were meant to be broken, and hellenism (that is, Greek culture, language and thinking) was especially successful at crashing everyone else's cultural party. Combine the power of Greek intellectual life with the swirling cultural milieu of the eastern mediterranean in the final decades before the birth of Christ, and we find ourselves in the situation where a Jewish writer, living in the Alexandrian capital of Egypt, composing Greek commentaries on the Old Testament (which had been translated from their original Hebrew into Greek) would become the primary architect for the application of Greek thought to the Hebrew/Christian God. The God of Moses could now be seen through the eyes of Plato, thanks to Philo Judaeus (15 B.C. to A.D. 50).

We know very little about the life of Philo except that his brother was the Roman-appointed governor of the Jewish sector of Alexandria, and that he led an embassy to the Roman emperor, Gaius Caligula, defending his community against charges of disloyalty.[20] Obviously well-bred and well-educated, he was an upper-class heir to the rich hellenistic, cultural heritage disseminated throughout Egypt by the Ptolemaic dynasty that was finally swallowed by Rome once Cleopatra lost Marc Antony to the sword of Caesar Augustus. Though Philo wrote volumes, there is no evidence that he had any significant influence upon his contemporaries, either Jew or

Gentile.[21] The preservation of Philo's writings is due entirely to the leaders of the Christian church a century after his death.

The earliest, public defenders of the Christian faith were men who had themselves been converted from other religious and philosophical backgrounds—Pythagoreans, Stoics, Platonists, intellectual, mystical searchers of various stripes. Extensive schooling in a diversified, Greek philosophical heritage would have been common background for them all. In Philo they found an intellectual compatriot devoted to reading the same sacred books as themselves. So, even though these early Christian writers did not need Philo's help in learning how to think like Plato or Aristotle, they certainly found his works a gold-mine of productive material for their fledgling enterprise of applying classical education to the interpretation of the Old and New Testaments. This alone ensured the preservation of Philo's work for posterity. Christian thinkers quickly adopted Philo as the standard exemplar for reading the scriptures and articulating Christian theology. Eusebius, the first Christian historian, tells a (fanciful) story of Philo visiting Rome and being converted to Christianity by the apostle Peter.[22] Origen, the second leader of the Christian academy at Alexandria, carried a complete set of Philo with him when he moved from Alexandria to Palestine in A.D. 233, single-handedly preserving his literature for future generations.[23] However, this popularity also seems to have sealed Philo's fate among his compatriots. The later Jewish rabbis, apparently finding it suspicious that his work should be so loved by their arch-enemies, the Christian apologists, decided it was better to be safe than sorry. Assuming his guilt by association, Philo's works were deliberately neglected and so consigned to historical oblivion.[24]

For his own part, however, Philo was true to the faith of his fathers. As a representative of hellenistic Judaism, he sought to take what he viewed as the best of two different worlds and to fuse them seamlessly into a compelling whole that might convince any thoughtful Gentile to believe in his Creator, the God of Abraham, Isaac and Jacob. Consequently, Moses became a wise man tutored in the great philosophies of Egypt, Assyria, Babylonia and, most importantly, Greece.[25] The Genesis creation account was retold entirely in terms of Plato's *Timaeus*.[26] What God had created in six days had been modeled after the pre-existent Forms, nurtured as eternal ideals in the divine reason.[27] In Philo's interpretation of Exodus, the God of Abraham, Isaac and Jacob metamorphosed into the unknowable, unchanging, incomprehensible God "of unspeakable Being" described by Plato.[28] Whereas, the original revelation of God's name in Exodus 3:14, "I am what I am" or "I will be what I will be," was meant to capture Yahweh's commitment to be endlessly faithful to an indestructible relationship with the people of Israel, Philo effectively identifies the Greek Septuagint translation of God's name, "I am the One who is" with Plato's eternal Being. The transmutation from a God of revelation into the God of philosophy was so thorough and complete that the fourth-century church father Jerome was able to say, "If Philo is not a platonist, then Plato is a philonist."[29] No one stood to disagree.

Philo devotes an entire treatise to defending the passionlessness of God in his book, *On the Unchangeableness of God*. Beginning as an exposition of Genesis chapter 6, he comes to verse 6 where God is said "to repent" over the creation of mankind. Yet, Philo wonders, "What can be a greater act of wickedness than to think that the unchangeable God can be changed?"[30] He is compelled, therefore, to find some other way to account for the biblical language. Though, in my opinion, he never does successfully explain what the author meant to say by claiming that God repents, he does account for the phrase by appealing to the literary device of anthropomorphism (that is, a description of God in metaphorical terms where he is compared to a human being). According to Philo, there are two types of people who read the sacred text. The first applies "sound reason" to understanding the truth of the divine nature; these people "are content with the bare conception of (God's) existence" and are not in need of such intellectual crutches as crude anthropomorphisms.[31] They are able to conceive of God in pure abstraction, understanding what it means for him to "exist himself by himself alone."[32] To these the scripture says that "God is not like a man."[33] The other sort of reader, those of "a duller and more sluggish nature," can only apprehend God through the limitations of changing physical perception; these folks need to be given pictures of God describing him in the more rudimentary, material terms they can comprehend. For their sake the scripture says that "God is like a human being."[34] He is described as a heavenly person with strong hands, burley arms, a kind heart and passionate feelings.[35] But none of that is intend to be taken as real. Obviously, a reader's spiritual development will cause them to outgrow the apparent deception entailed in ever actually believing any of these metaphors, whether they are *anthropomorphisms* (that is, instances of God described by the language of human form), or *anthropopathisms* (instances of God being described by the language of human emotion). As pure, unchanging Being, God obviously has neither body, parts nor passions.

We see that long before anyone calling himself a Christian had begun to read the Bible, interpretation of the Jewish scriptures and explanation of the Jewish God were being done according to a Platonic template. We have no idea how many hellenistic Gentiles may have been attracted to Judaism because of Philo's work, but we do know that many later Christians would be attracted to Platonic theology due to Philo's influence. The seeds had been planted for what would eventually come to be called the Alexandrian school of theology.

THE POWER OF NEGATIVE THINKING

Tracing the developmental influence of Greek philosophy throughout the early Christian church would require more than one lifetime and much more space than is available to us here. Fortunately, we can arrive at an adequate picture of the course of this development, and why we need to address it even today, by comparing the work of only two early church leaders: Clement and Tertullian. These two highly educated men, both brilliant children of their age, charted significantly different courses for how Christian faith and learning were to shape an acceptable description of God. They may even offer lessons on how we ought to tackle the subject today.

According to ancient tradition, Clement (A.D. 145?—215?) was born into a pagan household in the city of Athens, queen of the ancient intellectual centers. He spent his early adult life wandering throughout the Greek-speaking provinces of the Roman empire, studying with a variety of religious and philosophical masters expanding his classical education. In approximately A.D. 180, he travelled to Alexandria and encountered the well-known Christian teacher, Pantaenus. For whatever reason, Clement became convinced that this new Christian teaching offered the clearest expression of the ultimate truth for which he had been searching. He quickly joined Pantaenus' school and began a new phase of his education. It was not a process of relearning as much as it was one of expansion. Clement remained convinced that Plato offered a true explanation of life, the world, and in fact, all of reality. In this regard, Plato and Christianity fit together perfectly, like hand in glove. Greek philosophy had always been God's gift to the world, and when properly understood, it was preparatory to the Christian gospel.[36] In fact, the Greek philosophers had developed their thought on the basis of what they learned from Moses.[37] Christianity was simply the completion of what God had long been doing through Plato and Moses alike; they were two streams flowing from the same fountain into a common ocean. Thus a proper Christian education required both faith, in the study of the holy scriptures, and reason, in the study of ancient philosophy, each in equal measure. Clement's educational philosophy was identical with Philo's at this point. And, given his choice of schools, it should not be surprising to learn that Clement was also the first Christian author to mention Philo by name.[38]

Clement had found his niche. He caught the attention of Pantaenus and eventually ascended to the leadership of what would come to be known throughout the empire as the Alexandrian school, respected by Christian and non-Christian alike. Posterity will always remember him as Clement of Alexandria, and his articulation of biblical teaching as seen through the lens of Platonic philosophy would become the overwhelming influence in Christian thought for centuries to come.

Like Philo before him, Clement applied the Platonic method of the *via negationis* to his explanation of God. Since there is no continuity between God and the world, deity can only be understood in terms of what it is not:

> God is not in darkness or in a place, but above both space and time, and the qualities of objects.[39]

> The Divine Being cannot be declared as it exists...[40]

> Advancing into immensity by holiness, we may reach somehow to the conception of the Almighty, *knowing not what God is, but what God is not* ... The First Cause is not then in space, but above both space, and time, and name, and conception.[41]

> God is invisible and beyond expression by words.[42]

God cannot really be described at all, at least not in the ways that we normally think of description. Naturally, like Philo before him, this also means that Clement must view all the anthropomorphic and anthropopathic language of the Bible as a condescending simplification of God's person into rudimentary picture-language. Clement explains that these images need to be interpreted allegorically, probing the spiritual truths resident inside the concrete descriptions. In this way, the student can learn to throw away the misleading, external husk which says that God has hands or emotions, and save the genuine heart of the matter pointing toward the Divine Mystery. Such revelation both reveals and obscures, simultaneously. The challenge is not to confuse the two sides of the process. Although this may sound rather complicated to the uninitiated, it is an unavoidable result of the mercy shown by God when he accomodates divine revelation to the human predicament.[43] Revelation is God's attempt to describe the indescribable, to make known the unknowable. We must learn to read and then to *un*-describe—to *un*-know—what has been imperfectly described and made known in human language.

It goes without saying, then, that Clement's new Christian God was also impassible (the technical word for "without passions"), as were both Plato's and Philo's portraits of the divine.[44] Clement also has occasion to highlight the way in which the question of emotions impinges upon the Platonic issue of divine unity. Remember that Plato emphasized that God is One, as opposed to somehow being complex or intra-personally divided (something Plato assumed was necessary for emotions to function). Clement wholeheartedly agreed on this point:

> God is ranked as the All, and is the Father of the universe. Nor are any parts to be predicated of God. For the One is indivisible.[45]

> God is one, and beyond the one and above the Monad itself...God who alone is God is also alone . . .[46]

In Clement's mind, passions equal disturbance, conflict, indecision—again, agreeing with Plato. Passions involve the type of emotional confusion that prevents people from completing the good that they intend. In the Greek mind-set, passion was not merely emotion; it was emotion run-a-muck, counter productive emotional disturbance that obstructed the rational pursuit of beauty and truth. So, for example, women hesitate and fail to follow through on noble sacrifices because of fear—fear, thereby, shows itself to be a destructive passion. Men are tempted to abandon their families in the grip of passionate lust—demonstrating that even so-called love can be a destructive emotion best rejected. Because these passions fight against the reasonable, enlightened decisions of the mind, not only are they incompatible with the one God who exists alone in simplicity,[47] but they are also incompatible with the life of the true believer. Because God is free from passion, God's people must aspire to passionlessness as well. Just as the Christian is redeemed from sin in this world, spiritual growth will increasingly unfold into liberation from human emotions:

> It should be granted that the affections . . . when produced rationally, are good, yet they are nevertheless inadmissible to the case of the perfect person . . . [The Christian] is compelled to become like the Teacher in impassibility. For the Word of God is intellectual . . . [T]he complete eradication of desire reaps as its fruit impassibility.[48]

Notice that in making this argument Clement has subtley associated the passions with sinfulness and imperfection in a way that will affect Christian thought for years to come. The notion of the true saint being the one who remains above the fray, untouched, unperturbed, immune to upset, serenely surveying the tempestuous storms of life from the sheltered harbor of God's passionless protection will be cultivated for centuries in contemplative traditions as the ideal of Christian spirituality. The passions are not mere emotions; they are the conflicted, combative desires that sabotage what is reasonable, right and true.

So far, Clement has not strayed very far from the pathway cut by his intellectual predecessors. He has synthesized Plato with Christian thought in much the same way as Philo had synthesized Plato with Jewish thought. However, at its core, Christianity is animated by one crucial distinction which, theoretically, could make all the difference between Philo and Clement: the incarnation—the belief that Jesus of Nazareth was God in the flesh. This doctrine is what set the first-century religious step-child apart from its ancient Jewish mother. Clement of Alexandria believed that Jesus was the God-man. And if God had become a human being—the One who was beyond space and time had actually come to inhabit time and space—then surely the question of whether or not God can experience emotions must be recast in an entirely new light. Or maybe not.

Actually, this would appear to be the place at which Clement's commitment to both divine revelation and human reason lead to unresolved conflict. On the one hand, he faithfully asserts that Christ really "suffered for us."[49] At least during the earthly period of his life, the Savior experienced the passions involved in being tried and executed. This admission of passion in the experience of the incarnate Son, however, still does not touch upon the question of divine impassibility *per se*; in other words, the eternal Father might still remain impassible while the incarnate Son suffers temporarily. And, in fact, so deep are Clement's Platonic roots that he cannot even allow himself to consistently say that the Son suffered in the flesh:

> Our Instructor is like His Father God, whose son He is, sinless, blameless, and with a soul devoid of passion; God in the form of man . . . He is wholly free from human passions.[50]

Granted, Clement's implicit connection of passion with sinfulness may require a more nuanced reading of such statements, but it remains to be explained how Christ could have truly suffered anything at all if in fact he remained devoid of any and all passion. Clement seems to be admitting his own intellectual difficulties with these questions when he finally settles upon a solution one can only call a benevolent, heavenly deception. At the end of the day, Platonic reason declares victory over biblical faith and Clement explains that Christ only appeared to suffer human frailties so that his followers would not suspect that he was anything other than one of them. God had played a spiritual shell game:[51]

> For He ate, not for the sake of the body, which was kept together by a holy energy, but in order that it might not enter into the minds of those who were with Him to entertain a different opinion of Him ... But He was entirely impassible; inaccessible to any movement of feeling—either pleasure or pain.

Others will eventually try to solve this dilemna by suggesting that Christ suffered and experienced passion in his body (or human nature), while in his spirit/soul (or his divine nature), he essentially remained impassible. At some points, Clement seems to toy with this idea himself. But it becomes apparent that he finally hesitates to allow Christ to truly suffer in any way at all, even in his mortal body. It is difficult to arrive at any other conclusion than that Clement compromises the content of the biblical message in order to accomodate the limitations of his philosophical tools. Rather than adapting a new tool, or creating a new philosphical or theological formulation which might do greater justice to the content of the biblical message, Clement finally surrenders the New Testament picture of Christ in order to save the integrity of his philosophical assumptions. In the mind of Clement, Jesus of Nazareth must be sacrificed for the resurrection of the Unmoved Mover.

IS PLATO THE ONLY CHEF IN THE KITCHEN?[52]

Tertullian was born soon after the middle of the second century in the northeast corner of North Africa, in the modern country of

Tunisia. His father was a soldier in the middle ranks of the Roman army who was at least wealthy enough to offer his son a solid, classical education. Tertullian received thorough training in rhetoric and law and eventually established a legal practice in Rome. There is no record of what eventually attracted the young, successful Roman lawyer to the Christian faith, but the church in Rome was at least a century-and-a-half-old by the time he arrived in the city. He undoubtedly found himself with numerous Christian contacts spread throughout the capital, and they eventually persuaded him to adopt their faith in Christ as his own. It was not long before he returned to his home in North Africa and became a leader of the church in the provincial capital, Carthage.

Tertullian differed from Clement in his attitude about the Christian appeal to Greek philosophy in biblical interpretation. He certainly was not anti-intellectual, nor was he even, strictly speaking, anti-philosophical. He was well-versed in philosophy himself and showed a personal sympathy for the school of the Stoics. But Tertullian was much less enthusiastic about the apparent benefits of this intellectual cross-pollination than were his Greek-speaking, Christian contemporaries (Tertullian wrote primarily in Latin as a leader in the western sector of the church). He was far less willing to grant philosophical presuppositions the status of self-evident truths than was Clement, his eastern contemporary. He certainly was a strong advocate of intelligent, reasonable investigation and debate, but Tertullian also clearly placed the greater priority upon the biblical text. God does not ask us to be unreasonable, simply to submit our intelligence to the authority of his revelation. In fact, the most important use of human intellect was in the proper interpretation of the scriptures. Tertullian explains his method in *A Prescription Against Heretics*:[53]

> One's aim is carefully to determine the sense of the words consistently with that reason which is the guiding principle in all interpretation.

If, at any point, philosophy and the Bible seemed to stand opposed to each other, the plain sense of the text must be honored as primary. Tertullian's brilliantly attentive reading of the Old and

New Testament text demonstrated that this did not require the Christian to be caught up in obtuse simple-mindedness. Yet, he does not mind the odd rhetorical flourish to declare his loyalties in words one would never find coming from Clement of Alexandria:

> Indeed, heresies are themselves instigated by philosophy... Away with all attempts to produce a mottled Christianity of Stoic, Platonic and dialectic composition![54]

> God's Son was crucified—this is not a matter for shame, because it is a disgrace; and God's Son has died—this is credible because it is foolishness; and he was buried and is risen—this is certain, because it is impossible![55]

Tertullian describes "the humiliations and sufferings of God" as another example of the foolish impossibilities necessarily believed by Christians. Since Christ was crucified and Christ is truly God, God was really crucified and genuinely suffered death. This fact makes it unacceptable for anyone to suggest that Christ only appeared to suffer, as Clement had attempted to do. To suggest that Christ's physical sufferings were fictitious or imaginary—in any sense, as being less than entirely real—was to imply that a part of the gospel message was a lie. And if a part, then why not the whole? In other words, if his bodily sufferings were an illusion, then why not his spiritual power as well?[56]

Tertullian was convinced that divine passibility—that is, God's ability to genuinely experience passion—was at the heart of the Christian message because he found it at the center of the biblical record. If it did not fit with Platonism, then Plato must be set aside. Keeping true to form, Tertullian did this very sensibly, not as a religious reactionary, but as a clear-headed thinker who offered a considerable rationale that any opponent must take seriously.[57]

First, Tertullian made important observations about the limitations of analogy and metaphor.[58] The anthropomorphisms of the Bible are imperfect attempts to offer limited descriptions about specific aspects of the nature of God. No such comparison is ever perfect, and we cannot assume that the original author intended an exhaustive one-to-one correspondence between the known human quality and the divine characteristic being hinted at in the comparison. We must appreciate the limits of analogy and not press them unreasonably or we will arrive at absurd conclusions. For example, we say metaphorically that a chair has legs. But no sensible person hunts for the chair's knees with a rubber hammer, expecting to find a reflex. We naturally understand that metaphor has limits. In much the same way, to describe God's behavior in terms of human emotions, as the biblical writers do, is not to suggest that God's passions are identical to our emotions in every respect. We must remain open to the possibility that it is precisely at those points where philosophical objections arise that we may be encountering the limits of the divine-human analogy:[59]

> By all these affections God is moved in that manner peculiar to deity, in which it is profoundly fit that God should be affected...

This argument becomes particularly relevant to the Greek hesitation to attribute emotions to God because emotions entail change. However, Tertullian reminds us that God is also by definition utterly unique. If God does experience emotions, they will be unlike any other emotions ever experienced by anyone else. More specifically, since people experience emotions in a life bound by time, it is to be expected that we may speak of our emotions as "changing" us over time. But, since God is eternal, his experience of emotion is free of the time constraints known by human beings. If we say that God cannot experience emotions without changing, then we are assuming that (at least, with respect to emotions) God is really no different than time-bound humanity. But this cannot be true, since God is unique and ought not to be prohibited *a priori* from experiencing emotions in a way appropriate to the divine.[60] Therefore, it is more likely that a unique God is able to experience emotional changes *without actually changing*, than it is that the deity would be restricted to a logical box of changelessness built by the Greeks.[61]

Second, Tertullian argues that God is the perfect model for personal behavior, not because the human form had been an eternally conceived ideal in the divine mind, as Plato suggested, but because God had created man and woman as his own divine image. Human beings are the *Imago Dei*. The Creator said in the first chapter of Genesis, "Let us create humanity in our own image." God is the original. We are the copies. Consequently, when trying to describe the nature of God the correct line of logical investigation ought to proceed from God to humanity not *vice versa*. From Tertullian's perspective, the sensible investigator does not try to explain God with reference to people, but attempts to explain people with reference to God:[62]

> It is absurd of you to be placing human characteristics in God rather than divine ones in humanity, and clothing God in the likeness of humanity, instead of humanity in the image of God. And this, therefore, is to be considered the likeness of God in humankind, that the human soul has the same emotions and sensations as God, although they are not of the the same kind; differing as they do both in their conditions and their issues according to their nature.

God does not possess human qualities perfectly. We possess divine qualities imperfectly. Though he does not say it outright, Tertullian seems to imply that human experience alone ought to make the existence of divine emotions self-evident. The real focus of the debate, therefore, ought to be in discovering how God's perfection makes the divine emotional life different from ours.

Finally, all of these observations led Tertullian to a view of divine revelation diametrically opposed to that of Clement. Remember that for Clement, as for Philo, when the scripture shows God to be like us, we are reading an inferior form of communication which requires a spiritual reinterpretation. Since God is actually nothing at all like us, such images must be viewed as an expression of divine accomodation that need to be read allegorically in order to be properly understood. However, Tertullian insisted that it was actually the similarity between God and humanity that allowed any sort of meaningful communication from God to be possible in the first place. Biblical analogies and metaphors are not evidence of an inferior step of accomodation on God's part; they are examples of the miraculous possibilities that exist for an intimate divine-human relationship between God and the *imago dei*. Without emotions, both in God and in us, there could be no communication because there could be no point of personal contact between heaven and earth:[63]

> God would have been unable to hold any intercourse with humanity, if God had not taken on the emotions and affections of humankind...

The incarnation of Jesus Christ—God become flesh—is the eternal reality of God made historically concrete. It was not a trick, not an illusion, not some heavenly slight of hand. It was not even out of character but was entirely in character for God to become one of us. Jesus offers the flesh and blood example of how a person can exercise the divine emotions perfectly, as God had always intended. Rather than being an embarrassment, like the drunkard black sheep of the family who is always hidden away at family gatherings, Tertullian makes God's emotional life an important bridge between heaven and earth, something to be openly embraced, for it gets us closer to the truth about both God and ourselves than philosophical contemplation alone ever could.

CHOOSING THE ROAD LESS TRAVELLED

It should be apparent that Clement and Tertullian offer two alternative schools of thought for anyone wondering whether or not God has feelings. The two schools will continue to play a serious game of tug-of-war throughout the history of the Christian church, but Clement's approach to the question eventually won the day. In later life, Tertullian became associated with an enthusiastic, renewal movement springing from Asia Minor calling for the rebirth of Christian prophecy. This movement, called Montanism, was judged to be far too passionately irrational for the majority of the early church. Eventually, the powers-that-be judged it to be heretical, and Tertullian's outspoken support of the group with its female prophetesses meant that the legitimacy of his writings were darkened by new clouds of theological suspicion. He was consigned to the ranks of dangerous thinkers. Augustine of Hippo, the fourth-century intellectual giant of the western church, remembered him as "Tertullian the heretic,"[64] even though Tertullian's pioneering explorations into the relationships between God the Father, the Son and the Holy Spirit would form the basis for the doctrine of the Trinity later adopted by the orthodox church.[65]

The ambiguous reception of Tertullian's views did at least mean that the majority of this writings were preserved intact (albeit, with warning labels attached); as a result, his investigations into God's emotions never completely vanished from the scene. He was also viewed sympathetically by a variety of later thinkers who shared his suspicions of Greek philosophy.[66] Yet, their periodic warnings against the dangers implicit in Greek thinking for Christian theology were like tiny handbells rung at the base of Big Ben chiming at noontime. The spectacle and grandeur of the all encompassing intellectual synthesis offered by the various schools of Greek thought finally proved irresistable. The juggernaut of acceptable theology stuck to the tracks of Alexandrian thinking and chugged slowly but steadily through the Christian church, despite the occasional rocks of protest thrown against it. God's unchangeableness became an all-embracing philosophical touch-stone for orthodox thought, without regard to possible nuance or biblical fine-tuning. Thus God also became *immutable* (meaning that there is no change in essential being); *omniscient* (God knows all things past, present and future, never changing in understanding or knowledge); *omnipresent* (God is at all places at all times, never changing location); and *omnipotent* (God has all power such that there is never a need to revise intentions). Granted, the Bible does make statements that might be construed as hinting at these formulations, but there is more than one way to interpret them. However, the importance of Greek metaphysics (the rational investigation of the nature of reality) had become so strong within the church that reconsidering these questions from the more biblical perspective of personal inter-relationship and divine faithfulness was not even considered an option. These philosophical concepts, now called the "incommunicable attributes of God," became non-negotiable planks in the platform of scholastic, confessional theology. Such scholasticism reigned within the church throughout the middle ages into the Enlightenment and the modern era. So, for example, in 1861 the well-known German theologian and university professor Heinrich Heppe published *Reformed Dogmatics*, a work intended to be a textbook for beginning theology students introducing them to a collection of what he considered the best historical examples of traditional theology. Turning to his chapter on the attributes of God, we find this definition:

> God is immense and great without quantity; good, true and righteous without quality; action without movement, merciful without passion; present everywhere without position.[67]

Platonism was more than alive and well. It had established its throne and was thriving in the nineteenth-century academy. This was how pastors were being taught to describe God to mothers and fathers in Sunday sermons; this was the lesson for children in mid-week catechism class. God still could not be described, except in his essence as absolute Being. He had no discernable qualities, characteristics or passions. A woman might go to Sunday worship searching for a personal God, but she would be asked to bow down before the ineffable, the unknowable, divine simplicity. The mature method of prayer was the *via negationis*. The First Cause and the Unmoved Mover were tenaciously ensconced in the church. Baptized, catechized, confirmed and now ordained, the ghosts of Plato and Philo had not only set up shop, offering their wares to the intellectually curious, they had taken over the household of faith and required that every family member commune with their spirits or be expelled. Is it any wonder that modern thinkers began to feel more oppressed than liberated by theological tradition? One cannot help but wonder what Feuerbach may have concluded had his theological schooling majored in the God of Tertullian rather than the God of Clement.

2

IN THE SHADOW OF LOVE

Why Would God Be Angry?

> *Even in anger itself there is also contained a showing of kindness.*
> —Lactantius
> *A Treatise on the Anger of God,* 16

> *There is a cruelty which pardons, just as there is a pity which punishes.*
> — Abraham Heschel
> *The Prophets,* 2.76

Perhaps you have heard the story about the tenacious outdoorsman setting out for a long-awaited weekend at his mountain cabin. Unfortunately, it began to rain as he drove his four-wheel drive into the mountains, and by the time he headed up the dirt cut-off to his retreat, a mudslide washed out a part of the road taking his truck along with it. He barely managed to escape with his backpack and a few supplies.

Not to be deterred, he decided to hike the rest of the way comforted by the fact that once he made the cabin he could easily build a fire and dry himself out. However, he had not gone far when he was overwhelmed by an avalanche. The backpack was torn from his back, and all of his supplies were lost. Luckily, he managed to swim out of the tumbling white current and saved himself, barely.

He was a stubborn man, and since he did not have much farther to go anyway, he pressed on consoling himself with the thought of sitting before a warm fire crackling in the stone fireplace, sipping a hot espresso. As he crested the last hill he anxiously looked ahead only to see the burned out shell of his cabin standing at the end of the road. It had been struck by lightning during the storm and burned to the ground. Tiny curls of smoke were rising from the still glowing embers.

This was the last straw. The man fell in a heap at the base of a pine tree. Hitting his head against the trunk, he cried out over and over again, "Why me, Lord? Why me?" Suddenly, the man was blinded by a brilliant shaft of light from the heavens. The clouds parted and the voice of God spoke loud and clear, "Because some people just tick me off."

Perhaps you and I can laugh at this story; others find it more difficult. While few of us may have actually heard an audible voice from the clouds, many have suspected that heaven's silence delivered the same message more powerfully than any epiphany. Fear about divine anger is nothing new, nor is the suspicion that our bad luck is evidence of God's bad temper. The ancients wrestled with these same suspicions about vindictive, unpredictable gods and asked similar questions. Only a brief survey of world mythologies is required to discover that men and women from the beginning of time have regularly tried to explain their personal misfortune in terms of capricious gods who seldom hesitated to take their frustrations out on unsuspecting humanity. In fact, the early Greek philosophers claimed this as partial motivation for rethinking the nature of the divine. If you do not like the gods you have, make new ones, or at least reconsider your interpretations of their role in life. A few, such as Epicurus, went so far as to find in philosophy a refuge from any and all gods, regardless of temperment. They may exist somewhere, but they viewed this world with placid disinterest. The Stoics were more moderate, suggesting that God may be benevolent but never angry; he might do us good, but he would never do us malicious harm. The majority, as we have seen, argued that God was free of all emotion, positive or negative. Whatever happened to us in the course of life could not be associated with either divine retribution or benevolence. God may discipline us through circumstantial adversity, but such lessons were for the benefit of society at large, to prevent the spread of evil; they had nothing to do with heavenly passions or concern for the individual. Plato, you remember, had argued that apparent changes in the divine-human relationship reflected a change on the human side alone. What might superficially appear to be God's anger was actually the outworking of a new human predicament where we suffer the consequences of our own behavior. God was not angry. We had been foolish. Any apparent change is ours alone. What we may interpret as God's emotional response is actually the practical outworking of our changing personal circumstances. It only appears as though God is doing us good or harm.

Of course, how the average man or woman in the ancient marketplace may have interpreted the confusing swirl of life's kaleidoscope, whether as good luck, bad luck, the random events of fate, impersonal cause-and-effect, divine blessing or punishment, is anyone's guess. You may recall that Socrates was publicly executed for his new, unorthodox way of thinking about the gods. I suspect that people have not changed all that much throughout the ages. Plato's neighbors probably would have reacted to this joke in much the same way as people today.

Over the years I have had numerous conversations with people who were honestly convinced that God's main purpose in life was to "get them," to make their life as difficult and uncomfortable as humanly—or, in this case, as divinely—possible. It is a minority opinion to view life as a closed arena, shut off from outside influences, where we simply suffer the impersonal blows of cause-and-effect. The more common reaction when tragedy strikes is to assume that God is playing games. A loved one gets sick and we wonder for which offense God is punishing us. Life becomes an unpredictable game of tit-for-tat with an irascible deity who not only keeps score, but makes sure that he evens the score whenever possible.

Of course, the Bible often does not seem to help much. All we have to do is turn to the Old Testament to find story after bloody story depicting what some would describe as an angry God of vengence and mahem, pitching heavenly fireballs, turning overly curious women like Lot's wife into salt-blocks, and renovating unruly cities like Sodom and Gomorrah into smoking wastelands. This Old Testament God appears to be a cosmic Gengis Khan, slashing and burning wherever he goes.

In protest, some decide to follow the example of the ancient philosophers and simply redefine, or even reject, those aspects of the traditional, biblical, Judaeo-Christian God which we find most objectionable. Anger has always been the most controversial of the divine passions and the most likely to be eliminated, even by those who might otherwise retain some sympathy for the idea of a passionate God. For example, Clement of Alexandria, while inconclusively eliminating emotion from God's personality, nevertheless refused to let go of the belief that God was full of love.[1] However, he did allow that love may show itself most clearly in discipline, so instances of apparent anger could actually be situations where God's love is showing itself in circumstantial correction.

Origen (A.D. 185-254), Clement's successor to the leadership of the Alexandrian school, was even more brilliant than his predecessor, equally at home in the Greek classics as he was in the Hebrew Old Testament. Attempting to maintain the philosophical legacy of his church tradition, Origen also argued that God was free of any and all passions—definitely anger, and seemingly, even love. Using what he had learned from Plato, Origen concluded that all instances—from scripture and personal experience alike—where God appeared to show anger, were simply God's dispassionate correction of human error.[2] The situation pinched because we were twisting against life's pinchers, not because God had fingers. Biblical language for wrath was a figurative—allegorical—description of the consequences for human disobedience. And, if we were wise students of life, we would embrace these painful circumstances as welcomed, disciplinary opportunities to rid ourselves of the counter-productive human emotions that lead us into such messes in the first place.

Granted, for some of us these solutions may appear enticing after a first reading, but further reflection should cause us to pause. In each instance, the elimination of divine anger is only the thin end of a wedge eventually leading to the complete obliteration of any and all emotional life from God whatsoever. Give this God of the philosophers an inch, and it will take a mile. The outcome of the trade-off is not simply an angerless God, but an impersonal God; not a God who takes only a positive interest in us, but a God who shows little if any interest at all. Like the naïve innocent who wishes for eternal life only to discover that by getting her wish she is consigned to a never-ending purgatory of continuous aging—arthritis, wrinkles, menopause and all—we ought to think carefully about what we are doing before permanently erasing anger from the list of God's desirable emotions. We may find that we want our God to be capable of outrage after all.

ASSUMING THE WORST: COMMON MISCONCEPTIONS ABOUT GOD

Some years ago, I was facing a particularly stressful personel problem at my job. I was trying my best not to bring work home with me, but we all know how difficult that can be. One evening after dinner my twelve year old son tentatively looked across the dining room table and asked, "Dad, why are you so mad all the time, lately?" You could have knocked me over with a feather. I was depressed, stressed and, probably, withdrawn. I certainly was angry with some people at work. But I was not in any way angry at my children. Yet, they were watching the outward expression of my inner emotional turmoil churning away and interpreting what they saw as anger directed at them! Believe me, we had a family conference then and there. I tried to explain the situation and reassure my insecure children as best as I could. Dad had some problems, yes, but my problems had absolutely nothing to do with them! Whether or not their anxiety began to melt largely depended upon the bonds of trust and confidence that had developed between us over the years. Hopefully, we would all relax.

Many of us regularly look at God in much the same way as my children were looking at me, guessing at a distant parent's mysterious emotional life. We hope for the best, assume the worst, and place ourselves as the central culprit. So, of course, if bad things are happening around us, it must be because God is angry with us. I once counselled a woman who was so extreme in her guilty self-examination that she honestly blamed herself for world catastrophes reported in the evening news. (I'm not exaggerating). Even though few go to that pathological extreme, many of us have journied some distance down a similar road. However, I would suggest that when we jump to these sorts of conclusions, we are as wrong about God as my children were about me.

Typically, we labor under at least three misconceptions about God which make such misunderstandings inevitable. Though these assumptions are seldom made public, they are typically lurking just beneath the surface of our religious psyche; and, not surprisingly, they all are rooted in the absence of trust and confidence.

First, we suspect that God's anger is *arbitrary and unpredictable*. We can never predict when, where, how or why the next lightning bolt will strike. Thus the continual questions: Why? Why me? Why here? Why now? You just never know when you might be the next one to tick God off.

Second, we wonder if at least part of the reason divine anger is so unpredictable is because *God enjoys getting angry at people*. After all, if there were no heavenly pleasure in the outburst, why does God seem to lash out so frequently? And if the root motivation behind God's tantrums is whimsical, personal pleasure, as opposed to some reasonable cause-and-effect response, then understanding such behavior becomes a bit like predicting what a drunk will do on his next binge. Isn't that why we call natural disasters "acts of God?" The supreme being just happened to decide that wiping out a few thousand family homes with a hurricane might be good weekend fun.

Third, we conclude that a God such as this should, at least, be *feared* and, if possible, *avoided*. Why would anyone want to have a relationship with a holy terror like the God of the Bible? I once had a friend who made it a habit to call his brother every day after school before walking home. He wanted to learn whether their father was drunk or sober that day. It was impossible to predict when the old man might be drunk (he did not necessarily wait for the weekends), and when he was drunk it was just as impossible to predict whether he would greet you at the door with a bear hug around the shoulders or a clenched fist across the chin. Needless to say, my friend was very choosey about which afternoons he risked sneaking in the back door, and it did not take many years before he decided never to return again. He was no sado-masochist.

These three questions—Is God arbitrary? Is God vengeful? Can God be trusted?—are answered intuitively by each of us in the course of life's daily routine. We acquire a backlog of experience and draw conclusions accordingly. The follow-up question, however, is not as intuitive; in fact, it can be down-right tricky: *Are my intuitions correct?* Or, like my children, do we need a first hand, corrective explanation from the Source?

GETTING TO KNOW A PERSONAL GOD

Personal relationships evolve through self-revelation. A recent acquaintance tells me about his divorce. I listen to his words, watch his facial expressions, read his body language, hear the catch in the bottom of his throat, and in the process I receive a personal revelation which—if handled carefully—will lead me into a deeper appreciation of my new-found friend. I may well hear second-hand reports about his divorce from others, and depending upon the source, that information may well be factored into my evolving appraisal; however, nothing can replace the first-hand information acquired by personal contact.

So it is with God.

Genuine insight into God's character must be the result of a personal encounter with some divine self-explanation. Naturally, we may debate the appropriate places to uncover this communication. Not everyone would agree that the Bible is a reliable source of dependable information about God. It is not my intention to revisit that debate here. I would simply suggest that the collection of religious writings which has inspired many of the richest literary and artistic acheivements of our civilization, and has historically prodded western society towards individual equality and human rights, merits serious consideration by any honest seeker after God. We need to think long and hard about the Bible and its historic presentation of Mosaic monotheism—together with all the unavoidable moral claims of the One who says there is only one, true God—before making any final commitments about the place of the divine in our lives. THE crucial Old Testament revelation of this deity appears in the Pentateuch, when Yahweh is revealed to Moses upon Mt. Sinai as a lofty and intimate God:

> God passed in front of Moses, proclaiming, "Yahweh, Yahweh, the compassionate and gracious God, slow to anger, abounding in love and faithfulness, maintaining love to thousands, and forgiving wickedness, rebellion and sin. Yet not leaving the guilty unpunished." (Exodus 34:6-7)

The relational God of the patriarchs, the redeemer who rescued Israel from Egyptian slavery, the eternal ethicist who exposed the naked, divine character to humanity in the giving of the law, this God is a multi-faceted Being exhibiting a complex emotional makeup that includes compassion, graciousness, love, faithfulness, and forgiveness—as well as a willingness to inflict punishment and to be angry.

Along with Tertullian, I suspect that if we ever hope to have a genuine relationship with a truly personal God, we must surrender our idiosyncratic attempts to custom-make a supreme Being according to our own plans. This is a religious dead-end that merely leaves us pondering our own reflection in a mental mirror. We must allow God to reach out and engage us in conversation, unveiling bits and pieces of the eternal personality in heaven's own timing. We must listen first; then and only then are we free to wrestle with what was said. We do not have to like what God tells us. We may finally want to reject heaven's overtures. But we cannot simply disregard the message. We have already seen that, for this very reason, Tertullian refused to sacrifice any of the divine emotions, because he took passages such as Exodus 34 seriously. Fortunately, Tertullian's method was not entirely buried after he had been tarred with the heretic's brush. He provided a useful model for an important 3rd century leader of the western church named Lactantius (A.D. 260?—320?), who became the first Christian author to tackle the subject of divine anger directly. His book, *A Treatise on the Anger of God*, offers a number of observations worth repeating, not just for the sake of historical curiosity, but because of their profound insight.[3]

Lactantius was no arm-chair theologian. He was converted to Christianity while teaching classical rhetoric in the palace of the Roman Caesar, Diocletian (A.D. 284-305), an emporer whose reign would implement one of the more intense periods of persecution against the Christian church, even though his own wife was a member of the faith. Lactantius made his convictions known and lost his position as a result; only his public reputation seems to have spared him from further consequences. Years of poverty and unemployment followed, giving Lactantius plenty of opportunity to consider the relationship between life's misfortunes and divine providence.

On the Anger of God begins by observing that the Bible reveals God as a "person" in possession of a *whole* personality. Drawing the analogy with human personality, he concludes that a God who could never become angry would be rather like an impersonal lump, not only immune to mistreatment but equally incapable of warming to goodness.[4] A God unable or unwilling to enforce correction would be similarly devoid of any comfort. However, anger is the inevitable shadow cast by the protective pillar of love. In a moment of unreflective passion, I once found myself charging like a crazed bull across the street in front of my apartment. I was marching into a potential battle-zone to confront a small gathering of neighborhood gang-bangers that had howled unsolicited cat-calls at my pregnant wife. Fortunately, they apologized and I was spared a visit to the hospital. I confess that I felt no shame over my anger (that may have changed had I been shot), though I would have been deeply shamed had I ignored the insults and quietly walked away. (I don't care if my Sunday school teachers did tell me to turn the other cheek). Love for my wife required her protection.

Similarly, Lactantius observed that any God who genuinely loved people would swell with protective indignation at anything that threatened their well-being, whether that threat originated from within themselves or something else:[5]

> The one who loves the good also hates evil, and whoever does not hate evil does not love the good; because the loving of the good arises from the hatred of evil, and the hating of evil has its rise from the love of the good . . . The one, therefore, who loves also hates, and whoever hates also loves . . . Because God is moved by kindness, therefore God is also liable to anger.

Though we may wish to find a substitute for the word hate, Lactiantius' point is well taken. How can we continue to speak about divine love if we will not allow God the appropriate vexation when evil attacks the beloved? God's anger is protective not offensive; always reactive, never unprovoked; always appropriate, never unreasonable or unexpected.

Of course, a loving anger may be as complex as love itself—disciplinary, protective, correctional, or instructive. At times, such anger may be expressed directly and actively, but at other times, it may be more passive or indirect. For example, there are those moments when divine anger may be moved to take direct action against evil, but the Bible also frequently describes *divine withdrawl* as the more severe expression of God's rebuke. To be left entirely to one's own devises; to be allowed the freedom of suffering all the surprising consequences of our foolish choices, without the unwanted interference of a God with moral expectations, this is the harshest version of heavenly punishment. Like a drug addict killing himself with hypodermic ecstasy, our insistence upon uninterrupted freedom will eventually drain our life away. So the Bible speaks in terms of God "hiding the face," "turning away," "allowing us to go our own way" (see Isaiah 64:7; Jeremiah 12:7; Ezekiel 39:23):[6]

> In a surge of anger
> I hid my face from you for a moment... (Isaiah 54:8)

> God's anger is being revealed from heaven against all human wickedness. . . Therefore, God handed them over to their own

sinful devices ... (Romans 1:18-28)

Imagine that you are waiting for a business flight in the airport terminal where you see a young mother with her six-year old son fidgeting and fussing, turning the waiting area into his own personal play-room. He runs over other people's newly polished shoes; spills his drink on a seething businessman's Armani suit; all the while remaining completely oblivious to the discomfort he is causing everyone. Initially, his frustrated mother tries to keep him under control in her own enlightened fashion, but she is powerless over the strong-willed terror.

"Eric, please sit down with mommy."

"No, I don't want to."

"Eric, do as mommy says now, please. You are bothering that man. Let's read something together over here."

"No, I don't want to read anything. Besides, he was in my way."

Finally, the embarrassed mother reaches out to grab her son by the arm.

The boy kicks his mother in the shins and screams at the top of his lungs, "No, you're not my mommy, and I don't have to listen to you!"

The frustrated woman turns beet red, sinks into her seat and begins to ignore her son's antics. He climbs up into a seat and peers over the shoulder of a businessman desperately trying to complete an overdue proposal on his laptop before the plane begins to board. Reaching over the man's shoulder, Eric says, "Let me try!" as he begins to bang his hand on the keyboard. The previous night's work is erased in an instant. Enough is enough. The man closes the computer, grabs the small boy by the shoulders, pulls him across his knee and gives him a sound spanking.

Through it all the boy's mother calmly continues to read her paperback. When her little boy comes to bury his wet, red face into her lap complaining about what the mean man has done, all she can say is, "I'm sorry, but you got what you deserved." She hopes that her son has learned a much needed lesson; next time she may not be close enough to watch out the corner of her eye and intervene if necessary.

Whether or not we agree with this woman's parenting style, there are those moments when, like the little boy, we get exactly what we deserve. How much better it would be to experience the discipline we need from the hand of one who loves us. But God, in respect for our freedom, will allow us to refuse to listen, in which case heaven's protection may be withdraw, leaving us to clean up the mess we so desperately wanted to make.

This is the biblical portrait of God. Divine love sprouts anger whenever the loved ones are threatened, even when the threat comes from within the beloved themselves. Sometimes, God intervenes to protect; at other times, heavenly discipline rumbles loudly; in still other moments, heaven is silent as we are allowed us to suffer our own fate. Yet, the Bible (especially the Old Testament) regularly assures us that we never need to fear because God never finds pleasure in anger for its own sake. In fact, God is incapable of anger "for its own sake." Divine anger is only expressed *for our sake* as God unleashes eternal love in as many ways as may be appropriate, whether tenderly or firmly, directly or indirectly, as protection or correction.

Even as an expression of love, God's anger is a last resort. In eight additional places, the foundational message of Exodus 34:6-7 is repeated to Israel:[7]

God is slow to become angry, but is overflowing with love.

The message is reiterated in other words, as well:[8]

His anger lasts only a moment,
but his favor lasts a lifetime...(Psalm 30:5)

Getting God's goat is a bit like launching a nuclear warhead. It is possible, and the effects can be serious, but it is also incredibly difficult. A missle launch by the U.S. government would always be preceeded by predictable protocols with abundant advance warning. There are multiple safety features coded into each of the launch sequences. Nuclear missles never just fly off the handle and neither does God, since the capacity for anger is simply a coefficient of a divine eagerness to patiently love even those who incite God to strike. Heaven's anger is as slow as molasses in January, but love is ready to overflow at the drop of a hat.

The New Testament book of I John, chapter 4, verse 8, says that "God *is* love." This is worth reflecting upon, for nowhere does it ever say that "God is anger." God is not Anger with an ability to love. God is Love with the ability to become angry. Love is the genus; anger is the species. That is no small distinction. There is a colossal difference between what a person *is* (as a matter of being, all the time) and what a person is capable of *becoming* (as an expression of emotion, temporarily). I *am* a father to my children, all the time, without exception. Nothing can ever change that bond between us. I may *become* happy, impatient, satisfied, or even angry with my children depending upon the circumstances of the moment, always as a coefficient of my paternal love. I am always a father who loves his kids, first and foremost: a happy father; an impatient father; a satisfied father; even an angry father, but always a loving father. Love is not just a set of clothes that God wears to church on Sunday; it is the heart and soul of the divine nature, the beginning, the end and everything else in between. Whenever we encounter God we are confronting the One who is all love all the time, always directed at being utterly in love with us. Our Creator may at times become temporarily disappointed, saddened or angered. But even in those moments we still encounter eternal Love: disappointed love; saddened love; angry love. But always love.

A JUST ANGER OR *JUST* ANGER?

The second crucial observation made by Lactantius concerns God's justice. The Creator is ultimately responsible for the oversight of creation. As actors on the world's stage, trying our best to get our lines right, we each eventually ask our own private questions about the source(s) of evil and the gross inequities through which we sometimes find ourselves plodding. Good people around us, friends and strangers alike, are sucked down by the undertow. We do our best to stay afloat, throw out the odd life-preserver and kick against the current, but all to no avail. As a result we wonder, Why must life be so unfair? Ultimately, the problem of evil remains a mystery, for both Lactantius and for us. But he does offer an important assurance: God is not just the Creator, God is the Creator who is just. We may question heaven's timing. The seemingly round-about manner of divine operations may drive us to distraction at times. But at the end of the day, when the timing is right—sometimes in the here and now, but more often in the distant future—God's righteous indignation will cleanse the world of filth. Heaven will punish those who made victims of the innocent. This Judge's anger will be just because his justice never overlooks a wrong. In the meantime, we are assured that our Creator has suffered with us as a parent agonizes over a suffering child.

As long as we insist upon excluding anger from God's emotional range, we are demanding that we be given a God who never becomes indignant over injustice. Our deity patiently overlooks rape, racism, prejudice and child abuse without developing an angry bone in his body (so to speak). Is this the kind of God we want? Would such a God be worth having? If a judge were to routinely set murderers and child molesters free, without a twinge of regret or a ripple of indignation, let alone outrage, we would lobby for his immediate removal from the bench and label him a moral aberration. Frankly, we are very happy to know that there are judges presiding over our courtrooms who are angered by injustice and faithfully administer the appropriate punishments. In much the same way, I (for one) happen to be attracted to the idea of there being a God in heaven who not only promises to one day defend the weak and punish the cruel, but also tells me that our Maker empathizes with those who are hurting and, consequently, is angered—yes, ANGERED—by the two-bit bullies, thugs, gangsters and dictators who cause so much pain in the world. Lactantius reminds us that silence in the face of evil is either tacit approval, laziness, or both. God suffers from neither:

> God is moved to both sides, both to favour when seeing that just things are done, and to anger when perceiving unjust things...[9]

> The one who is altogether unmoved (by evil) either approves of faults, which is more disgraceful and unjust, or avoids the

trouble of reproving them...Therefore, restraining one's anger in the case of sin is a fault.[10]

The options are rather straightforward: a God who never became angry would never—could never—be angered by injustice. And, ultimately, any Creator who was unmoved by injustice in the creation would be an unjust God. We have a choice. We can accept either (1) a God who never becomes angry because of a rank indifference to right and wrong, or (2) we can have a God who knows what it is like to be outraged because of a deepseated sense of justice and personal commitment to our welfare.

When homeless people freeze to death on our city streets while community leaders play political power games, bickering over zoning disputes for new homeless shelters, God becomes angry.

When the court system works in such a way as to allow the rich and the guilty to go free simply because they can afford high priced lawyers and endless appeals, while the poor and the innocent are sent to jail, half-heartedly defended by overworked and underpayed public defenders, God becomes angry.

In 1995 I read a news story about Major Donald Lowry. Major Lowry was an Air Force F-15 pilot who died when his fighter plane crashed during take-off. An investigation revealed that there was a design flaw in the connecting rods of the elevator flaps on the F-15. Thomas Mueller, the veteran mechanic who had performed the maintenance work on Major Lowry's plane, had made a mistake in the connections, an oversight that resulted in the crash. The Air Force accused Mueller of negligent homicide and began court-martial proceedings.

However, there was just one problem. This particular design flaw in the F-15 appears to have been widely known for quite some time. There had been a number of other, identical accidents. Numerous recommendations had been made to correct the design problem and to educate the mechanics accordingly. However, the upper eschelons of the Air Force chain of command had never taken any corrective measures to solve the problem. Apparently, they were unwilling to admit that such a major mistake had been allowed to go into production in the first place.

During Thomas Mueller's trial both Major Lowry's wife and father had stepped forward in his defence. They argued loudly and compassionately that the real negligence lay, not with this one mechanic, but with the Air Force powers-that-be. But, however much the dead man's family pleaded for the accused, the court-marshall proceeded.

The trial came to an unexpected halt just one day before the Muellers' nineteenth wedding anniversary. On that morning, Thomas Mueller put a gun to his head and pulled the trigger. Mr. Mueller Sr. found his son's note: "I know I am going to heaven, and in heaven I cannot hurt anyone else. Not even by accident." Case closed.

Why did God allow this double tragedy to happen in the first place? Why does it so often seem that we are left trying our best to salvage whatever we can from life's wreckage, rather than receiving the advance help we needed to avoid the crash altogether. It seems as though God could spare everyone a lot of unnecessary outrage, and many of us a lot of avoidable tragedy, if heaven would only offer more preventative intervention when we needed it the most.

I do not know the answers to those kinds of questions. Who can guess why Donald Lowry and Thomas Mueller, as well as countless other good and decent people, are allowed to die before their time? I do not know. But I do know this: I know that unless there was some aspect of this case that has never made it to the press, Thomas Mueller was warmly embraced that day by the long arms of his loving God, the same God who will one day see to it that all innocent victims are vindicated while all self-satisfied power brokers are torn down and forced to face their guilt. God guards the bar of eternal justice as the defender of the weak, and even though we may not understand the timing, our Creator has declared that there will come a "day of wrath" when every hidden record will be set straight and every whispered appeal will be proclaimed from the mountain tops. It will be an unveiling of righteous anger. The Old Testament prophet Zechariah (7:9-12) writes:

> This is what the Lord Almighty says, "Administer true justice; show mercy and compassion to one another. Do not oppress the

widow or the fatherless, the alien or the poor. In your hearts do not think evil of each other." But they refused to pay attention... So the Lord Almighty was very angry...

BLINDED BY ANGER OR SEEING THINGS CLEARLY?

Talking about righteous indignation is one thing, truly exercising it is another kettle of fish. The human experience of anger can be so convoluted that we quite rightly hesitate whenever anyone else tries to justify their own angry outbursts. There is a human tendency to be confident of one's own self-understanding but highly suspicious of everyone else's. As a keen observer of human nature, the famous eighteenth-century English lexicographer Samuel Johnson once said, "Justice is my being allowed to do whatever I like. Injustice is whatever prevents my doing so."[11] Cynical, but true. Because I can see myself in Johnson's analysis, I know that I am easily able to convince myself that my outbursts of anger are reasonable, while yours are self-serving and out of line. Perhaps God is involved in the same game? How do I know that God is to be trusted, in this respect, any more than anyone else? Righteous indignation could be a pious façade covering God's temper tantrums, rationalizing what is actually religious coercion keeping the faithful blindly, stupidly in line.

Here is the problem. We all tend to see what we want to see in precisely the way that we want to see it. Nowhere does this become more complicated than in the way we perceive God and ourselves. Finding satisfactory answers to the questions raised by divine anger requires that at some point we gain a clear understanding of both God's character and our own motivations. We come back to the question of divine revelation. What does God reveal of the divine character? Am I able to receive this message? And how does a relationship with this God illuminate my own inner recesses? Pursuing answers to these questions will eventually show me that, whether I admit it or not, I have a definite tendency to place more trust in myself than I do in the Creator. This is why talk of divine justice may continue to sound hollow, whereas taking matters into my own hands rings true to my ears. However, before dismissing divine justice as hogwash, we need to take a risk of ruthless self-examination. Do we really see life's landscape all that clearly? Is it possible that our latent scepticism over God's so-called righteous anger is actually our own unwillingness to listen to a voice other than our own?

Tertullian's warnings ought to be remembered. God does not possess human qualities perfectly, people possess divine qualities imperfectly. Imagining God's emotional experience to be identical to ours is as misguided as thinking that the angels actually posed for the portrait painted by Michaelangelo on the Sistine Chapel ceiling. Anthropomorphisms say that God is like us, but only to the extent that God can be like us. All God-talk is ultimately metaphorical by necessity.[12] Since God is (1) unique and (2) dissimilar to us, we can only describe deity (1) in terms of comparisons (with dissimilar objects) that consequently, (2) will suffer distinct limitations (due to God's uniqueness). When we say that God is a "father" we do not suppose that the eternal Spirit has actually had sexual intercourse in order to share heavenly DNA. When the ancient Israelites called God their "king" it was a comparison with a known example of authority; no one conceived of God literally wearing a golden crown embedded with jewels. Every metaphor has limits. Biblical metaphors are limited by God's limitlessness; they are flawed by divine perfection. Yet, they do effectively describe something. The challenge is to figure out what that something is and move appropriately from metaphor to reality. This is done, partly, by reading the body of biblical metaphors about God wholistically. None of them stand alone. Some are more frequent and extensive than others.[13] Each interpretation sends trajectories of possible meaning in various directions, all of which intersect the possible meanings of every other metaphor in the collection. Some of these intersections are complementary and strengthen one another—God is called a father and a shepherd, both of whom are known to "care for their sheep" with their lives. Other comparisons seem to be incompatible, suggesting certain limits intrinsic to the images themselves—God is both a rock and one who becomes angry. Obviously, at this intersection God's rock-like qualities cannot include emotional disinterest, as would be intended when describing someone as having a "heart of stone."

How, then, can God be conceived of as an angry rock? Obviously, when intersecting with an emotional metaphor, interpretation of the rock imagery must be taken in another direction, one that will allow for a rock with passion. Finding the right solution is a matter of sensitivity to context. The context will provide the help needed to discover that the rock metaphor, in this instance, is intended to depict God as reliable, firm, a secure foundation that will never erode. This supplies an image easily combined with other emotional metaphors—in this case, God's anger is never fickle but always firmly based on solid, predictable character.

So, we return to the earlier question: what assurance can we have that talk of God's righteous indignation is not simply a ruse distracting us from the fact that divine anger is actually quite arbitrary? Remembering Tertullian's words, we again bump up against one of the limits of this particular metaphor. As Lactantius said:[14]

> There are some affections to which God is not liable, such as... fear, avarice, grief, and envy...God is not liable to these because they are vicious affections; but as to those which belong to virtue...inasmuch as they are worthy of the divine power, Deity has its own affections, both just and true.

Human emotions have been twisted and new ones, never intended by God, have been added to the mix. So the goodness of love can be perverted by insecurity into possessiveness and a desire to control. Unwanted interlopers such as envy and arrogance grow like weeds in life's compost. But these kinds of emotive confusions are the exclusive domain of humanity. God's heart is never confused because divine emotions are never anything less than perfect.

In fact, one of the reminders that the Bible itself is aware of these subtle distinctions in metaphor makes its point by contrasting divine anger and human vindictiveness. Confronting the problem of a rebellious people who deserve to be punished, the Old Testament prophet Hosea reminds Israel that their God will not lash out at them in spite; in fact, before they are punished, compassion has already begun to reign in anger:

> My heart is changed within me;
> all my compassion is aroused.
> I will not carry out my fierce anger,
> nor devastate Ephraim again.
> For I am God, and not a human being—
> the Holy One among you.
> I will not come in wrath. (Hosea 11:8b-9)

The limits of this particular anthropopathism are explicitly identified precisely in the way God's perfect emotions (in this case, anger) are to be distinguished from the imperfections of human emotion. Human anger may have occasion to drip with hidden bile, but never God's. Lactantius affirms that God is "never angry except with those who deserve it."[15] Mankind might flex anger unjustly but not God.[16] Heaven reaffirms that the Creator is not modeled after our twisted image every time the eternal Judge exercises restraint, refusing to lash out, ensuring that any eventual punishment is executed appropriately in the proper measure at the proper time. Here, also, is a partial answer to the haunting questions about delayed justice. What we may interpret as apathy, callous indifference towards wrong-doing, is actually divine patience ensuring that heaven's anger is just. No one but God can foresee all of the ramifications that may elicit such hesitation. The tangling of human anger with spite, like two different-sized pieces of string knotted together in the kitchen junk drawer, offers one more reminder that God cannot be measured by human standards. Knotted anger is the only kind we know. It is one thing God will never know.

Of course, some old fashioned theological purists (like my caller in chapter one) may continue to object that it is the very uniqueness of God that must preclude anger from the divine character—anger of any sort, whether perfect or imperfect. Never mind the earlier arguments about love and justice. If God is to remain God, deity must be able to rise above every negative impulse. The Creator ought to be capable of confronting even such conundrums as injustice without ugly complications. An angry God is an oxymoron, however positively we massage the definitions.

Such persistent questions only underscore how difficult it is for the human mind to step outside of its own experience and entertain even the theoretical possibility that there might well be an independent reality out there somewhere that is not determined by human necessity; that there might be a place where anger could only be experienced as a positive force used for good every time. Granted, there is no *a priori* reason that the human relationship with God should not exclude anger. But aside from the fact that the Old and New Testaments fail to describe such a relationship, the suspicion lingers that this kind of argument is rarely being driven by the engine of pure reason. It seems more likely that there is a deep-seated personal motivation involved. I would suggest that we intuitively understand that, at one time or another, WE have been guilty of the very sorts of behavior that merit God's anger.

Think about it: Few of us balk at the idea of a crusader-God or a social-activist-God who defends the innocent and punishes the oppressor, but we have significant reservations when we encounter a ruler-God, a God with expectations requiring obedience. That particular God sounds to us less like a savior and more like a control freak. We want our religion (especially in America) to be liberating not confining, personally fulfilling not restrictive. And so, at last, we think we have found an iron-clad reason to paint this God as the mean-spirited puppet master we always suspected. But, before settling on that solution too quickly, we should stop for a moment and ask ourselves a few final questions:

First, are there *no* circumstances under which a person has a right to expect another's obedience?

Second, is it *never* right for such a person to be angered by another's disobedience?

One of my earliest childhood memories involves a severe scolding from my mother when I was about five or six years old. She had taken my younger brother, my sister and myself on a shopping trip one afternoon in my father's blue '56 Chevy. She had one last stop to make at the end of an exhausting day. She pulled into the parking lot and, I'm sure, just like any harried mother, slowly weighed the options: on the one hand, she could take the time and effort to bundle up three cranky children, maneuver us through the crowded produce aisles and out the check-out line in a rickety, three-wheeled shopping cart, or she could take the brief risk of leaving us alone in the car while she rushed in to do the errand herself. She decided to take a chance. However, before dashing off she gave me firm instructions on what I was not to be doing while she was away. First, I was not to wake up my brother or sister. Second, I was not to touch anything. No knobs, dials, switches, handles, wheels, latches, levers or buttons. Nothing. I was *especially* not to touch one little knob that could be pushed into the dashboard and then popped back out with the opposite end glowing bright red. Whatever I did, don't touch that, she said!

Off she ran.

What do you think I did? You guessed it. Before my mother was even out of sight, I pushed that knob into the dash. I figured it had to be something special if my mom was so intent upon denying me the pleasure of its company. While she was away I would quickly enjoy a few stolen moments with that bright red glow.

My mother's banging on the car door window took me totally by surprise. I had become so enthralled with burning holes in the front seat with the cigarette lighter that I had not even noticed her frantic return. Don't ask me why my five year old mind thought that tattooing black, concentric circles in my father's upholstery would be a worthwhile project. I just did. Doubtless, at the time I believed I had a good reason for doing what I did, although the horrified look on my mother's face quickly told me that she was not about to agree.

After more than 40 years, I still have a foggy mental image of the severe scolding I received (and probably a spanking, too). Mom was mad, and she made it very clear that burning holes in the car seats was a good way to set the car on fire, turning my brother, sister and myself into smoldering memories for two grieving parents. I learned that there was good reason behind my mother's instructions. I had disobeyed. Her anger was justified. I deserved to be punished.

There are situations in which it is quite right for one person to expect another's complete obedience. Furthermore, it may be very reasonable for that person to become angry when the other disobeys. The relationship between request and response becomes intensified when the parties are bound together by parental love and youthful dependence. This is the context of the biblical vocabulary of divine anger. In another example, the apostle Paul addressed a fledgling first century church in the Asian city of Colossae, warning:

> Because of such things as sexual immorality, indecency, lust, evil passions, and greed, God's anger will come upon those who do not obey. (Colossians 3:5-6)

What kind of a parent dispassionately stands by watching her child play with a loaded gun and does nothing? Whether we know it or not, there are certain kinds of activities that burn gaping holes in the human soul, leaving deep, ugly scars which can eventually ruin us altogether.

Just ask the woman who only recently discovered that her husband has been cheating on her.

Talk to the CEO whose unrelenting pursuit of higher profit margins has cost him his family.

Visit the intravenous drug user who has passed on the AIDS virus to her newborn infant.

I can vividly recall the moment a psychologist helped me to realize that my insecurities were driving a workaholism that was threatening my marriage, and I see that I am often the insolent child engaging in the kinds of destructive behaviors damaging to those I love, as well as myself, that can make my loving Creator angry.

As surely as divine love requires anger at injustice, I am often the one who deserves to be pulled up short. Pain is invariably inflicted by someone, someone who becomes responsible for someone else's suffering. The gas chambers at Auschwitz did not build themselves, and it was not just a few who failed to protest the atrocity looming large next door. We have all heard news stories of incidents in one of our major cities where a woman is attacked on the streets at night. Dozens of neighbors hear her screams for help. They are average citizens just like you or me, washing their hair, watching television, reading a good book, and overhearing a violent assault in the dark alley below their bedroom window. The victim's muffled moans float through the air as she pleads for someone, anyone, to call the police. Yet, no one calls. No one moves a muscle, at least not to call 911, although a few do move to the windowsills to catch a peek at the commotion in the shadows just before pulling their window closed. They are afraid to get involved. There are only a few fleating moments of nagging guilt before the witnesses remind themselves that this crime does not concern them, and they ought not to intervene. But their silence binds them to the attacker in cords of moral insouciance, making them all accomplices. In how many crimes are we each complicit?

None of us can dodge life's left hooks forever. Eventually, everyone gets clipped. Eventually, we all must shoulder some measure of responsibility for the multitude of selfish, indifferent sleights that have added to the weight of the world's burden. Each of us has earned the title "Guilty." Lactantius observed:[17]

> God cares for the world; it follows that God cares for the life of humanity and takes notice of the actions of individuals and earnestly desires that they should be wise and good. This is the will of God, this the divine law; the one who follows and observes this is blessed by God. It is necessary that God should be moved with anger against the one who has broken or despised the eternal and divine law...

From our limited vantage point, it is impossible to foresee the long-term, potential damage of our behavior. We may try to argue that our actions are a private decision, making God's public warnings an unreasonable intrusion. However, my five year old mind could never imagine the potential connection between playing with cigarrette lighters and a '56 Chevy inferno. Yet my mother saw the connection, and because she loved me she warned me and punished me accordingly. Because I learned to trust her judgment and to do my best to avoid another spanking, I never played with a cigarette lighter again. And I thank her for her love.

Trust and guilt are at the heart of our discomfort over divine anger. Can I trust God only to flex those anger muscles justly? And will I stop denying my own culpability? But we are afraid of what might happen once we let this genie out of the bottle and admit that God has good cause to be angry.

Ironically, the solution to this fear is made available only by granting the very conclusion that we so desperately try to avoid. We must swallow the medicine if we want the cure. Admit that God does have both the right and the reason to be angry. Believe it or not, this is a positive step in the right direction, for we also recall that the God of the Bible only becomes angry because of a wholehearted devotion to:
- what is right
- our best interests
- a personal relationship of complete loyalty

Once we allow that God's anger can be legitimate, we also open the door to experiencing the eternal passion of a dogged commitment to love us in spite of ourselves. We deserve anger, yet we receive love. This anomaly is something the Judaeo-Christian tradition calls *grace*. Exactly how a God who supposedly loves justice pulls this one off—allowing the guilty to go free—is the focus of the next chapter.

3

DESIRE AND DISAPPOINTMENT

What Happens When God is Rejected?

God is not of such a nature as to need a friend...
he is too perfect to think of anything else beside himself.
—Aristotle
Eudemian Ethics, 7.12.15f

I made him just and right,
Sufficient to have stood, though free to fall.
—John Milton
Paradise Lost, 3.98-99

Age teaches lessons younger hearts could not fathom. I am learning this myself as a parent of teenage children, but I first saw it clearly as a graduate student working the evening shift in a local nursing home. I was a nurse's aid assigned to the wing known as the infirmary. Our residents required full-time care either because of terminal illness, dementia or some serious physical infirmity. I fed people dinner while wiping the drool from their chins; I changed diapers, cleaned dirty bed sheets and watched not a few die in their lonely helplessness. I was always amazed at how few ever had visitors. There was little if any connection between the elderly men and women I fed and the rest of the world. Where were their children, their grandchildren, their friends and neighbors, I often wondered?

One afternoon I arrived at work and began my routine of collecting dinner trays for the evening meal. I noticed a new woman seated in my section, hunched forward in her feeding chair, the table locked down to prevent her from falling out. She was sobbing, not loudly but deeply like someone trying to smother an inarticulate despair. I inquired at the nurse's station, wondering if there was something I should know about this woman before attempting to feed her dinner. I learned that she had arrived that afternoon. She had walked in on the arm of her son who explained his subterfuge to the nurse on duty, signed the required forms and drove away. Apparently, he and his wife had gone to visit his mother and offered to take her on a family outing in the country. Thinking that she was going for an afternoon drive and picnic with her grandchildren, she eagerly climbed into the back seat of the car. She was confused when they entered through the front doors of the nursing home, thinking that this was, perhaps, where they would pick up the children. It was not until her son turned and said goodbye that she began to grasp what was happening. That was when she started to cry; she had not stopped since. As far as I know, she never had a visitor in all the years I worked there.

Relationships can be painful. Abandonment. Betrayal. Unrequitted love. These are all a part of the human story. The more intimate the relationship, the greater the prospects of heartache when something goes awry. In fact, the relationships that mean the most to us are the very ones that can become most tragic. When you give your heart away to another human being, whether a spouse, a child or a friend, there are no guarantees that it will ever be returned intact. Of course, some of us respond to our first broken heart by swearing that we will never entrust ourselves to anyone else ever again. But we soon learn that in this life there is no such thing as true intimacy apart from emotional risk. Affairs of the heart know no guarantees.

DESIRE AND DISAPPOINTMENT

When we refuse to take such risks we shut the door on any possibility of experiencing true love. Every parent risks eventual abandonment in the infirmary wing where they will be fed and clothed by rough handed strangers earning minimum wage. Perhaps if more young couples squarely faced that fact, we would see a decline in the birth rate, but I doubt it. Hope springs eternal in youthful passion and inexperience, just as cynicism grows like moss through the cracks of broken lives.

Most of us forge ahead by optimistically insisting that brokenness is not necessarily terminal. We justify our persistence by deciding that the benefits of loving relationships, however fragile or temporary, make all the risks worthwhile. We become wiser, more discrete and less naïve; we come to relationships with fewer expectations and learn how to anticipate the storms before they hit. Sometimes the power of love itself simply makes it impossible for us to walk away. My grandmother, for example, married and ran away from her family's Nebraska farm when she was twenty-two years old. She spent the rest of her life with the same abusive alcoholic who had swept her off her feet. While many today would no doubt label her dysfunctional or codependent, she insisted until her dying day that she had simply found the love of her life and that the good times more than compensated for the bad. I suspect the truth lies somewhere inbetween.

Love is always risky because it is only exercised in freedom. While this insight may not make personal relationships any less confusing, it might help us to appreciate the necessity of the risks involved. Winning someone over with a magic potion that destroys his or her will to resist is not a romance story. If Romeo had kidnapped Juliet and forced himself upon her, we would continue to weep for her suicide but certainly not for his. If the future is good to me, I will one day anticipate happy visits with my grandchildren because I know that they visit me willingly, not because their parents force them (at least, not always).

Our deepest loves are the ones we enter and maintain freely. This is no less true of a relationship with God than it is of our connections with family and friends. We are discovering that the God of the Old and New Testaments is first and foremost a God of relationship who desires both to love and to be loved freely. When that reciprocity fails to take place God is as broken hearted as the mother abandoned by her own children.

CAN GOD USE A FRIEND?

At this point, it will not be surprising to learn that neither the Ideal Good of Plato nor the Unmoved Mover of Aristotle had any need for friendship, and so the theological traditions that eventually found guidance in their philosophies gave scant attention to the possibility of genuine reciprocity in the divine-human relationship. As the supreme Good, God is immune to change because deity is immune to the effects of any and all outside influences.[1] God is perfection, neither requiring nor seeking interaction with anything or anyone else. The most explicit philosophical treatments of this theme are found in two of Aristotle's ethical treatises, the *Eudemian Ethics* and the *Nicomachean Ethics*, dedicated respectively to his most faithful pupil, Eudemus, and his son Nichomachus who fell in battle in the prime of life. Substantial portions of both works are devoted to the nature of true friendship in all its various forms and expressions, including the friendship between a superior and an inferior, such as the connection between a master and a servant or a parent and a child. Of course, the ultimate relationship of this sort would be the relationship between God and a person. What does this brand of friendship involve?

Aristotle makes it clear that the exchange of benefits in such relationships are disproportionate, the superior party always receiving less benefit than the subordinate:[2]

These friendships then involve a superiority of benefits on one side, which is why parents receive honour.

That is, since children are entirely dependent upon their parents and unable to reciprocate in kind, they offer what they can, such as respect to their mother and father, instead of the more valuable commodaties like wisdom and protection that they receive. The greater the disparity between the two parties, the less mutuality can exist between them, and the less we are able to talk about true friendship at all. The individual's approach to God is the ultimate example of such an inequitable relationship:[3]

> It would be ludicrous if one were to accuse God because he does not return love in the same way as he is loved.

The Unmoved Mover is so far beyond the individual that he remains indifferent by definition. The infinite difference between God and humanity means that true friendship cannot exist between them:[4]

> God is not of such a nature as to need a friend...God's perfection does not permit this; he is too perfect to think of anything else beside himself.

A genuine response to human initiative, even human devotion, would involve God in the inferior process of change, something that is impossible for perfection. Friendships enhance life. Each party gains something from the innumerable, subtle contributions of the other. By reaching out to another person, we implicitly admit that our lives can be augmented, even improved. By accepting the offerings made to us, we tacitly acknowledge that we were not yet entirely complete. Yet, Plato insists in *The Republic*:[5]

> Things which are in the best condition are least liable to be changed and moved by something else...the strongest and healthiest is least altered.

Since God is by definition the strongest and healthiest of all things, the divine being derives no benefit and makes no response to the overtures of would be friends.

Early Christian thinkers could not express themselves quite as bluntly on this score as did their Greek teachers, since the sacred scriptures do *occasionally* describe the divine-human relationship as a friendship. The Old Testament prophet Isaiah portrays God referring to Israel as "the descendants of Abraham my friend" (41:8).[6] The prophet Jeremiah recounts a prayer addressed to God that begins, "My Father, my friend from my youth..." (3:4). (However, the context could be taken to suggest that these words indicated a failure to take God seriously). Even though such Old Testament references are sparse, the New Testament provides a new development in Jesus' own habit of referring to his followers as "my friends" (Matthew 11:19; 26:50; Luke 5:20; 7:34; 12:4; John 11:11; 15:13-15; 21:5).

The Judaeo-Christian God had always been a God of covenant; that is, one who makes a gracious commitment to be permanently connected to people come what may. The tradition made it clear that this connection had come through divine initiative. God had extended an arm in order to make Abraham a friend. In the ancient Near East there were a variety of types of covenants, generally involving personal commitment between a greater and a lesser party, but one option included mutual friendship. Consequently, early Christian writers could not oppose the application of relational language to God as forcefully as they had withstood any use of the language of emotions. But the strange, hybrid result was a nod of the head towards the theoretical possibility of friendship with God, while the possibility of genuine reciprocity—that is, a relationship in which God is as affected by us as we are by God—continued to be staunchly avoided. By in large, the majority was satisfied to pray to the God of the philosophers who may occasionally don the cloak of friendship, but never truly becomes a friend or partner to anyone.

GOD MAKES A MOVE

Even the most superficial reading of the Hebrew Bible introduces us to a strange new world of divine-human interaction that only coheres with Plato and Aristotle by the most overwhelming feat of mental gymnastics. "Only through arbitrary allegorizing was later religious philosophy able to find an apathetic God in the Bible."[7] Nowhere is this conceptual disjunction illustrated more clearly than in the Old Testament book of Exodus, chapter three, the *magna carta* of ancient Judaism. Israel had suffered in Egyptian bondage for four hundred years. This is the moment when God selects Moses to lead Israel to freedom. In appointing Moses to this task, however, God first invites him to enter into a personal relationship wherein they will speak to each other on a first name basis.

> Yahweh said, "I have seen the misery of my people in Egypt. I have heard them crying out...and I know their pain. So I have come down to rescue them...I will be with you." ...And God said to Moses, "I will be what I will be. This is what you are to say to the Israelites: 'I Am has sent me to you.'" (Exodus 3:7-8, 12, 14)

God introduces himself to Moses as Yahweh, a word most Hebraists agree is based upon the Hebrew verb "to be." Our best guess at the word's meaning is to translate it as "I am what I am" or "I will be what I will be." Within its original setting, this enigmatic identification finds its significance in the divine promise to always "be with" Moses and the people. Naturally, this curious name—I will be what I will be— prompts the question: *what*, exactly, will God be? The answer appears from the context: God promises to *always be with you*. "Yahweh" is the moniker of one whose heart beats with an undying commitment to personal intimacy. The Biblical ideal is engagement not detachment, sympathy not apathy. Unfortunately, for the divine name to be based upon the verb "to be" was an unexpected boon to ancient philosopher-theologians. As early as the 3rd century B.C., when the Hebrew Old Testament was first translated into Greek (a work known as the Septuagint or LXX), the Hebrew "I will be what I will be" had been rendered into the Greek "I am the One who is; the Being One." The designation of inter-active relationship had become a term for absolute being. It did not take long for God's commitment to relational fidelity to be thoroughly buried beneath metaphysical speculations groping after the eternal nature of unchanging, divine Being. The One who promised to always be *with us* was quickly transmuted into the One who always *Is*. The first God reaches out for intimacy; the second most easily stands alone.

Yet, there still should have been a glimmer of insight available to the careful reader. It is one thing for the president of the United States to say that he "feels your pain." (Personally, my instincts tell me that he just wants your vote). It is another matter altogether for the Creator of the universe to insist that human suffering has been taken into the eternal heart such that our anguish has been experienced and heaven has been moved, not to lobby for our vote but to reach out and to heal us of our brokenness. Yahweh is not only moved by but also shares in our pain. This God is not the Unmoved Mover who simply Is; this God is the Most Moved of All who actually comes down. How can we avoid the dynamic, emotional interaction of this story? God does not simply appear to relocate in relation to Moses; the claim that "I have come down" is not a sympathetic circumlocution disguising the fact that it is really Israel that has "gone up," as Plato, Aristotle, Augustine and Thomas Aquinas would have us believe by their stories about immovable pillars. No. This is absolutely not like Socrates shrinking (in appearance) beside a growing adolescent. This is the authentic pathos of a personal God who loves people so profoundly that the future of the divine being is willingly surrendered to the slings and arrows of outrageous human relationships.

The emotional payload of God's promise becomes especially weighty within the context of human unpredictability. God's decision to choose us is counter-balanced by our indecision. Like any frantic child, we are always free to wiggle out of God's arms and push ourselves away. Israel does this quite often. It is within this give and take, the ongoing thrust and parry of God's coming down to be with people who regularly choose to run and hide, that God's pathos becomes wedded to our liberty. All throughout the history of the Christian church those occasional leaders who were least infatuated with the legacy of Greek philosophy have continued to hold onto the centrality of such personal interaction with God, an interaction made real by the human ability to choose for or against their Maker.

Let me mention a few examples.

Irenaeus (A.D. 120-202) was the bishop of Lyons and Vienne, responsible for the oversight of the church in what is now southern France. He suffered through the persecution of the Christian church ordered by the Roman philosopher-king Marcus Aurelius in A.D. 177 witnessing the horrific torture of men and women from his congregations. Originally from the coastal city of Smyrna in southern Asia Minor, Irenaeus grew up in a Christian home that invested him with a lifetime passion for the Old and New Testaments. Though given a good education in his mother tongue, Greek, he had less affinity for philosophy than for the study of the original teachings of the apostles. He sat at the feet of the generation that had known the original followers of Jesus of Nazareth, and he worked to maintain and clarify their traditional teachings for future generations. In his major work, *Against Heresies,* Irenaeus consistently maintains the authenticity of personal free-will because it is essential to the individual's experience of a truly reciprocal relationship with God. Without personal liberty there can be no accountability "nor precious communion with God."[8] For example—and this is my example not Irenaeus'—if my dog only comes when called because I am tugging on the rope tied around its neck, I cannot honestly say that it is obediently responding to the sound of my voice. In much the same way, Irenaeus understood God to be waiting patiently for a good-faith response to heaven's good-faith offer of love. Human beings are not animals on a leash, but neither is God a mute bystander dispassionately watching his loved ones aimlessly wandering through the minefields of life. We have been given our freedom for a purpose; we are free to choose in favor of God.

It should come as no surprise to learn that Tertullian echoed Irenaeus in maintaining an appreciation for real human interaction with God.[9] His reasons were similarly rooted in the freedom of the will: the Creator had endowed humanity with freedom of choice in order to fulfil the promise of divine communion. God chose to love us. Heaven now waited for us to similarly choose to return that love. God is not aloof to the outcome, but yearns for us to respond.

GOD WANTS YOU ENOUGH TO LET YOU GO

My wife and I met at the University of Montana. I was a sophomore; she was a freshman. By the end of Terry's first academic year, when the tree-lined streets of Missoula's college district were budding explosively with splashes of springtime green, we both had decided that we wanted to spend the rest of our lives together. It would be some time before making any formal announcements to our families, yet with the approach of our first summer separation I already knew that there was only one woman I needed to see again in the fall.

A friend of Terry's had gotten her a highly paid job in an Alaskan salmon cannery. I was attending summer school at the University of Washington, eager to finish college sooner rather than later. While I knew we both would stay plenty busy, I was nervous. All my previous experience with women had taught me that summer separations invariably pulled the plug on love's respirator leaving a "do not resuscitate" sign over another of my ill-fated relationships. I had always been a hopeless romantic who perpetually thought he was in love with somebody. I knew the drill. In May you both swear fidelity. By September you just swear.

I remember the periodic swells of anxiety that first summer apart. I know I pulled straight As in all my courses largely because my only distraction from the terrible loneliness was feverish devotion to my schoolwork. The largest measure of my anguish was the simple pain of separation. Our love still enjoyed the morning glow of poetry (most of which I hope has been lost over the years) and daily letters (although I still insist I wrote more than she remembers). However, I would be lying if I said that the sum total of all my angst was born of such noble yearning. A significant part of me was much more crass. I was insecure. After the lights went out at night I could easily image Terry meeting someone else, an Alaskan lumberjack with biceps like Mt. McKinley who could easily make her forget the neurotic egghead back home. I was jealous and nervous and fearful as well as hopeful and trusting and expectant, all at the same time. Neither of us had tried to talk the other into changing their summer plans because we knew, at least as a decision of the will if not a firm conviction of the heart, that if our love was to last a lifetime, it would have to persevere through a litany of unpredictable separations, good, bad and indifferent. This summer was just a testing ground. We dutifully maintained a pen and ink lifeline between us; I have never before been such a faithful letter writer. But we also understood that we needed to let each other go, trusting that when and if we came back together the reunion would be fueled by a freely felt, mutual desire. I will never forget the overwhelming exhilaration when I first saw my future wife returning to me that fall, her long black hair and whinesome smile inviting me to wrap my arms around her in the Seattle airport. I actually leapt into the air and blurted out her name. We were together again because we each wanted to be with the other.

The Judaeo-Christian tradition has always placed a premium upon the individual's freedom to choose for or against the God who wants to be with us. Irenaeus,[10] Tertullian,[11] Clement of Alexandria,[12] Origen[13] and even the magisterial saint Augustine,[14] to mention only a few, all testify to the importance of personal choice in one's relationship with God. This freedom is inherent to humanity since it is part and parcel of what it means for us to be created in the "image of God" (see Genesis 1:26-27):[15]

> Man was constituted by God to be free, master of his own will and power; indicating the presence of God's image...

To be human is to be free. Even Augustine (A.D. 354-429), the brilliant north African bishop who loved Plato almost as much as the scriptures and was to lay down the theological foundations for the Reformation doctrines of eternal election and predestination,[16] consistently maintained that God never coerces anyone's response to his grace:[17]

> Indeed, to yield our consent to God's call, or to withhold it, is—as I have already said—the function of our own will.

This individual freedom to choose for or against God was typically used to answer the longstanding questions of theodicy, that is to explain the mystery of evil. Tertullian, for example, went on to argue that the only way for God to eliminate wickedness from this world was to divest humanity of its freedom. The power to choose was a two-edged sword that brought either life or death, depending upon how it was handled. The goal to which every human longing unwittingly aspired was connection with the Creator, a connection God eagerly made available but would never force. He waited to be chosen, like the little boy out for recess hoping that someone, anyone, would finally call out his name for the softball team. Unfortunately, we regularly make a litany of other choices, skipping over God like the third grade runt we think can't hit but, unbeknownst to us, can run like the wind. These other decisions invariably bear the destructive fruit of our selfishness and ignorance because our disconnection from the Creator leaves us with no moral compass. We are like isolated ships set adrift with no navigator, no sexton and no morning star. We exercise our freedom in the dark, moving in all the wrong directions; bruising our psychic shins against moral outcroppings we could never see, we continue to reach blindly for our own interests while ignoring God's offer. This is the moral dilemma posed by human freedom. Stripped of our freedom, we lose both our humanity and any opportunity to genuinely walk with God.

GOD AS A PATHETIC RISK-TAKER

The biblical story is a record of God's search for people. Having taken the risk of setting us free, the Creator now patiently looks for ways to reunite us. This is what I mean by the divine pathos. God engages in our lives, moving in rhythm with us across life's dance floor. Whether we waltz, cha-cha, do the mamba or the twist, we find that we are periodically swept up by a strange, dynamic, new partner who anticipates our every step and gently urges us to ascend to the next level by surrendering our need to lead. This dance of give and take between Creator and creature, Lover and beloved, wherein God circles through history making moment by moment adjustments in the pursuit of a relationship with you and me, this is the outworking of God's pathos. No apathetic God would ever surrender to such vulnerability, but the pathetic God of the Bible surely does.

Such divine pathos provides the underpinnings for all human significance. I used to have a friend who restored model T Fords for a hobby. I once asked him how much his latest restoration was worth. "Whatever I can get for it," he replied. "It's only worth what the highest bidder will pay." Well, God has decided that you and I are worth all that heaven has to give; a blank check has already been written for each of us. God is not the Ultimate Cause but the Ultimate Concern.[18] And in focusing all the eternal concern upon you and me, God invests us with an ultimate significance that, we

DESIRE AND DISAPPOINTMENT

can be sure, will always be a determining factor in every decision God ever makes about anything.

No one has ever expressed the mystery of divine pathos more profoundly than the hasidic rabbi, scholar, philosopher, and theologian Abraham Heschel. Born in Warsaw in 1907, he became a philosophy professor first in Berlin and then Frankfurt. Arrested by the Gestapo in 1938, he was placed in a Nazi detention camp and deported to Warsaw, as were all Polish Jews at the time. Miraculously, he was granted an American visa through the Hebrew Union College in Cincinnati and emigrated from Poland in 1939, just six weeks before the Nazi invasion, powerless to help the family he had left behind. Heschel's father had died when he was a boy, but before the war was over he would also lose his mother and much of his extended family to the extermination camps. Yet, rather than view the Holocaust as evidence for the death of God, as did so many others, Heschel clung to Yahweh, the God of Abraham, Isaac and Jacob, as his only hope for any meaning in life. As he wrestled with these issues, he concluded that life's meaning could only be found in knowing the God who suffered with his people. To Heschel's mind, the greatest dilemna facing the human race was not the problem of evil but the problem of finding a meaningful relationship with the Creator.[19] Evil itself arose like a phoenix from the absence of just such a relationship. A lifetime of immersion in the Hebrew Bible brought Heschel to an inescapable conclusion: the key to a genuine faith in God was the appreciation of divine pathos:

> God does not reveal himself (sic) in an abstract absoluteness, but in a personal and intimate relation to the world. He does not simply command and expect obedience; he is also moved and affected by what happens in the world, and reacts accordingly ... man's deeds may move him, affect him, grieve him or, on the other hand, gladden and please him.[20]

Nowhere is this dynamic interaction between God and humanity portrayed more poignantly than in the numerous scenarios where the Old Testament describes Yahweh as "having a change of mind" or "being filled with regret" over the developments in creation. When God confronts the egregious degeneration depicted in

Genesis 6:5, where "every human inclination was only evil all of the time," humanity has slid into a moral morass having once and for all abandoned the divine arm ready to steady its step. Wrestling with a world that now willfully stands in complete antipathy to everything the Creator had originally intended, Yahweh groans.

> The Lord was sorry that he had created humanity on the earth, and God's heart was filled pain. So the Lord said, "... I am sorry that I ever made them." (Genesis 6:6-7)

The declaration of divine sorrow is the unveiling of God's disappointment over human rebellion, not that people have disobeyed some ethical standard or code of conduct, but that they have willfully rejected their Maker. Older translations such as the Authorized Version of the King James Bible typically translated God's "being sorry" as a "repentance" or a statement of "regret," as if God now saw the need to correct some unforeseen error in the creation. However, insofar as such translations imply the need for God to correct a mistake, they do not quite capture the proper sense of the word. The mistake is not God's but ours. God does not need to be corrected; we do. Therefore, God's regret is actually a profound disappointment over the disjointedness that has invaded creation's original harmony, infusing the world with an alien, moral tension that must be rectified if the cosmos is not to fly apart. God is "grieved" even "broken-hearted" over humanity's disinterest in their relationship. God's grief is the coordinate of human evil. Brokenness begets brokenness. Yet, only one side of the breach is able to initiate a healing while hoping that the other will respond. Consequently, it is up to the Creator to take the first step, to reach across the jagged chasm, to work for a realignment of some sort that will eventually put things right between us once again, reaffirming creation as it was originally intended to be. It is in this sense that God's "mind is changed" by the developing circumstances.[21] The Creator freely makes deliberate adjustments and readjustments in order to reestablish relational harmony. Insofar as these adjustments are precipitated by our running away from God, they are steps that grieve God deeply, tearing large gashes in the divine heart, filling God with pain (Genesis 6:6).

You may recall that Genesis 6 is the offending text that had inspired Philo to compose his book *On the Unchangeableness of God* in which he argues that the description of God having second thoughts is simply a divine accomodation to the inferior spiritual sensibilities of those readers who may have "a duller and more sluggish nature."[22] However, once we forgive Philo for mistaking an insult for an argument, we may also point out that this assertion simply cannot withstand the impartial examination of all the biblical evidence. There are numerous occasions throughout the Old Testament storyline where God is said to reconsider a prior decision and then to adopt a different course of action—in other words, to change. For example, God "retracts" the Israelite kingship from Saul (I Samuel 15:11, 35). Twice God "relents" in punishing Israel because of the intervening prayers of Moses (Exodus 32:12-14) and the prophet Amos (Amos 7:3-6). There is a significant category of passages where the divine decision to punish is altered by God's own love and compassion.[23]

> The Lord will judge the people but will have compassion on them when their strength is gone. (Deuteronomy 32:36)

> The Lord took note of their distress and heard their cry...and relented out of great love for them. (Psalm 106:44-45)

Such compassion is God's "change of heart" (compassion, changing, and relenting are all the same Hebrew word) in not punishing rebellious Israel unduly but ending their chastisement once they return in repentance. This is a clearly articulated, fundamental principle of God's relationship with humanity. Like any responsible, loving parent, God will correct rebellious children when they self-destructively rebel, but will also freely "repent" of that judgment once we turn away from our disobedience (Jeremiah 7:5-7; 18:7-10; Ezekiel 33:13-16).[24] God's word to Israel is often conditional, taking the form of "If this...then that...But if the other.... then these..." The choice is ours. No good parent finds any pleasure in punishment for its own sake but eagerly retracts the harsh consequences once the child has learned her lesson. Herein lies the enticement of the alternatives offered by each "if...then" clause. This repeated evidence of God's compassionate willingness to change strategies is heaven's testimony that such punishment really does hurt God more than it hurts us.

Of course, Philo and his modern descendants are quick to point out the equally large body of seemingly contradictory passages which say that God is not like human beings who change their minds.[25] However, reading these passages in context will quickly reveal that they either pertain to a specific historical decision which God says will not be retracted,[26] or they offer a reassuring confirmation of God's complete dependability.[27] Just as we discovered in chapter two that divine anger is unlike human anger insofar as it is not volitile or unpredictable, in much the same way we see that God has made a faithful determination to be consistent in always following through on whatever has been promised to Israel. In other words, God will never do one thing while saying another; it is in this sense that God never changes.

I have read of studies suggesting that most of the lies we tell in our lives happen at home, and most of those lies transpire between parents and children. A father promises to take his son fishing and then catches the next plane out of town for an unexpected business trip. A mother promises to help her daughter choose a prom dress, but with her recent promotion, she never manages to find the time for an afternoon's shopping. Such behavior, if persistent and not merely periodic, will eventually teach our children that we are unreliable people who cannot be taken at our word. We change all the time, in all the wrong ways, saying one thing and doing another. But this is exactly how God is not like us. God never breaks a promise; in this respect, the divine heart will never change. On the other hand, that very faithfulness also makes our Creator consistent enough to make any necessary adjustments whenever a new tack is required in developing our ongoing relationship. The parent who adjusts his travel plans or rearranges her work schedule in order to keep a promise to a son or daughter makes the changes necessary to remain unchangeably reliable. Breaking your word is one thing; speaking a new word in the process of remaining true to a loved one is altogether different. While Philo's devotion to Plato blinded him to this distinction, we are fortunate enough to have modern voices such as Abraham Heschel's to help us understand that it is in fact the unchanging constancy of God's commitment to love us that makes divine change the historical sign of eternal faithfulness. God is always ready to tear a page out of the cosmic day-planner if that is what it takes to keep a rendezvous with you.

We might expect that such a central aspect of the divine character would poke its head through God's self-revelation in a variety of other ways as well, and we would be right. Without going into great detail, let me briefly mention three additional pieces of evidence demonstrating that God remains open to genuine reciprocity, honoring our freedom while simultaneously making the adjustments necessary to ensure that we are never outside the orbit of divine love.[28] First, the Old Testament prophetic books are replete with divine questions suggesting that God is at least profoundly disappointed, if not genuinely perplexed, by the refusal of certain people to stop their running.

> What can I do with you, Ephraim?
> What can I do with you, Judah? (Hosea 6:4)

> Why do my people say, "We are free to go our own way; we will not come to you any more"? (Jeremiah 2:31)

> What else can I do over the rebelliousness of my people? (Jeremiah 9:7)

Such questions are the outbursts of divine sorrow and frustration. Most of us will immediately recognize the familiar tone of parents at their wits end, locked in a desperate tug-of-war with a strong-willed child who simply refuses to listen. Trying to explain away God's questions as mere rhetorical devices does not really solve the problem, since we have already seen that every metaphorical device must ultimately point to some reality behind the words. Whether rhetorical or not, we must still give some account of the divine situation that prompts these musings.

Second, on five different occasions God refers to the future as genuinely uncertain, expressing a hope that "perhaps" the world will respond as hoped.[29] By uttering this perhaps, God reaffirms our freedom of choice. For example, having informed Ezekiel of the message he was to bring to the people of Israel, God concludes:

> Perhaps they will understand even though they are rebellious. (Ezekiel 12:1-3)

God makes a similar comment to the prophet Jeremiah where the divine perhaps intersects with God's eagerness to have a change of heart:

> Perhaps they will listen and every one will turn from their evil ways so that I may retract my punishment. (Jeremiah 26:2-3)

God certainly knows how to respond to any and every eventuality; nothing catches the Creator by surprise. Or does it? Granted, "the word 'surprise' is a highly symbolic form of language when applied to God, but it indicates something true about God's knowledge of creation."[30] The divine perhaps suggests that, whereas God may anticipate all future possibilities and have a calculated response to each and every one, it is not at all clear how we will actually respond to the various offers God makes to us. For God to foresee everything that might happen is not quite the same as God's foreknowing everything that actually does happen.[31] However, relationships as we know them unfold as one person offers and the other responds, each uncertain of what the other may do next. It is in this sense that the Bible depicts God entering into relationship with us. Our Creator waits for us to respond to heaven's overtures and is genuinely chagrined at the human propensity to reject divine love in order to self-destruct. The equivocation, the uncertainty, evoked by God's "perhaps" captures this perpetually surprising component in the divine-human relationship: we remain free to reject that which is best for us. The game of life is never rigged. Choices are always real. No matter how many times God is scarred by our rejection, no matter how many times we injure ourselves by going our own way, God never becomes numbed to our foolishness, nor does the divine sorrow ever overwhelm heaven's commitment to honor our freedom to choose.

Finally, God frequently consults with individuals before making any final decisions about the future enlisting human thoughts and actions as important factors in determining the next course of action. The most ancient example is found in Yahweh's consultation with the covenant partner Abraham over the possible destruction of Sodom and Gomorrah, cities that had become archetypes of rank debauchery.

> The LORD said, "Shall I hide from Abraham what I am about to do . . . ? No, for I know him . . ." (Genesis 18:7-22)

Abraham enters into a bargaining process with God that dramatically influences the final shape of God's decision. We have already seen how Moses occupied a similar role, pleading on behalf of an idolatrous Israel before the throne of God, finally diffusing the impending punishment. Eventually, such a give-and-take relationship appears to become a normative feature of every Old Testament prophet's responsibility.

> Surely the sovereign LORD does nothing without first revealing the plan to the prophets. (Amos 3:7)

This is not simply a description of God downloading an unalterable blueprint to some underling who must then execute heaven's design in every detail. This is an invitation to collaborate. God is willingly yoked to people who willingly listen and respond such that the future unfolds as it is jointly decided by God and a willing partner. God remains open to prayer, petition, requests, protests, objections and arguments to the contrary.[32] While this is not a guarantee that we will always get our way in the debate, it is an honest declaration that heaven's doors are always open to outside influence. As with any artist, the Creator is free to collaborate. Rogers did not have to work with Hammerstein. Lennon was free to write songs without McCartney. But each chose to create music with a partner, and the results are wonderfully distinctive melodies immediately recognizable to the modern, Western ear. Similarly, God is free to work, to relate and even to change in whatever fashion God alone may choose to change in relationship with divinely ordained partners in the historical, creative process. I am certainly no McCartney to God's Lennon, but you and I are the collaborators with whom God has chosen to compose life's symphony. Why not cooperate and drink in the lush harmonies that will weave their way throughout creation's chorus?

LIVING WITH OUR DECISIONS

The infirmary wing was not the entirety of the nursing home where I worked while studying for my master's degree. At the opposite end of the long L-shaped complex was a residential wing where the majority of our patients lived. The office of the activities coordinator has centrally located among these residents who were offered a busy schedule of social events and group outings, often to the casinos on the other side of the nearby Canadian border. To see these wheeled gangs of elderly men and women come and go you would have thought that they had entered a second childhood and were now making up for lost time. They laughed and danced, dated and teased. Only when they became seriously injured or deathly ill were they removed from the residential wing with its social calendar to the infirmary where all movement was at a minimum. These two ends of the facility were as different as night and day. Few people who entered the infirmary left under their own power. Occasionally, a patient would recover and return to her room at the opposite end of the building, but this was the exception rather than the rule. The nurses and doctors sent patients to my end only as a last resort after all else had failed. No one lived in the infirmary by choice; all were there by necessity, by someone else's decision, and in most cases, it did not take long for hopelessness to complicate their already gloomy prognosis.

The difference between the two wings was one of choice. The majority of residents sharing a wing with the activities coordinator had chosen to spend their final years in this nursing home. Perhaps it was not everyone's first choice, but even some choice is better than no choice at all. The occupants of the residence wing did not necessarily have any more contact with outside family or friends than the Alzheimer's patients I clothed and fed each day, but at least they were experiencing the life they had selected for themselves. My patients were always the pawns being moved about by some other hand, such as disease or family. Whether a patient felt herself to be a pawn in the game of life or a real player seated at the table made all the difference in how she responded to the surrounding circumstances. Players almost always found the inner resources needed to make healthy adjustments to life's unexpected moves. While those who believed they were only pawns inevitably succumbed to the debilitating complications of anger, bitterness, melancholy and despair.

God has chosen to take the risk of loving you and me. Yet, more than a few of us have, at one time or another, abandoned our Maker at the front door of the local, psychic nursing home; and in our disregard, God has suffered rejection. At no point in our discussion, however, have I intended to suggest that God is merely a helpless victim of circumstances. Let's not imagine the Creator with drool running down his chin waiting for an aide to take notice and wipe his face clean. God does not suffer our abandonment helplessly. God is able to suffer abandonment because of the choice made in the act of creation to become subject to such possibilities. There is a world of difference between these two conditions. Whatever restraints God may now experience are self-imposed.[33] Creation and self-restraint become simultaneous acts for the Creator. In wanting a relationship with someone else, God creates a space for the other to occupy.[34] God grants us freedom and then voluntarily abides by the limits that our freedom impose. Consequently, God may at times be a victim, but God is never victimized. Victimization is the result of helplessness, but God's suffering is always active never passive; God is subject to it but never subjected by it. Because God has chosen to risk suffering in and through our possible rejection, that suffering is never the final power over the divine heart. When suffering becomes sovereign over the truly helpless, such pain easily gives birth to bitterness and despair. My infirmary patients typically gave up and surrendered themselves to this black hole of hopelessness. But since God is never helpless, such bitterness and despair are never factors in divine sorrow. Sadness yes, hopelessness no. Consequently, while God grieves our loss, there is never any lashing out; no quest for revenge; no plans to get even.

God's decision to take this risk of personal relationship also helps to explain why the Bible so often describes God's disappointment as the combination of love with anger. God does not simply suffer eternally as if it were an intrinsic part of God's nature to always and forever be in pain; nor does God perpetually share in the history of human suffering as if the divine nature were an infinite sponge of continuous empathy. No. God suffers in personal response to the specific, historical instances of our saying "No" to heaven's offer of intimate relationship. In saying no to God, we willfully reject the very love we were created to enjoy. As a result, God is both heartbroken and angered, much like the parents of delinquent children described in chapter two. How many parents can idly stand by and dispassionately watch their children throw their lives away? In the right circumstances, true love demands a certain anger. Our rebelliousness evokes both the pain of rejection as well as the upset that elicits punishment from God. This, too, is the consequence of the divine decision to allow us the freedom to choose. Divine anger "is an aspect of the relative autonomy which (God) gives to mankind. It is the darker side of human freedom."[35] Both parties must be willing to accept the consequences of that freedom. The anguish resident within God's disappointment is the commingling of an eternal love that will never die with a momentary anger that is repeatedly provoked and simultaneously contained.

> How can I give you up, Ephraim?
> How can I let you go, Israel?
> My heart is changed within me;
> all my compassion is aroused.
> I will not carry out my anger...
> For I am God, and not man... (Hosea 11:8-9)

Of course, many of us would emphatically protest that, while we may not be following the traditional, religious party-line handed down from our parents or our upbringing, we have not abandoned or rejected God. Far from it. We are, in fact, more serious about our search for God than ever before. The only difference is that now we are seeking God in our own way, according to our own understandings. In this pluralistic, modern world where we are surrounded by a multitude of spiritual choices and alternative world-views—eastern, western, traditional, avant-garde, new age, mystical, pagan, and self-help—surely it is only right we each construct a personalized spirituality that meets the needs of our own individuality. Isn't this the opposite of rejection? Isn't this taking God more seriously than ever before?

How we answer such questions will depend upon whether or not we accept the notion that God has the right to be jealous of us.

4

GOD AS JEALOUS LOVER

Is Divine Pathos Pathological?

> The framer of this universe...was good,
> and what is good has no particle of jealousy in it.
> -- Plato
> *Timaeus*, 29c

> Even if He exists, I say, "Farewell to God," if He is of such a nature that He feels no benevolence or affection towards men.
> -- Cicero
> *The Nature of God*, 1.124

Chris has just received a frantic phone call from her childhood friend, Marcia. In between the tortured sobs, Chris hears Marcia describing a surprise encounter with her husband downtown that afternoon. Marcia had just parked her car and was walking towards her favorite store for some last minute shopping when she unexpectedly saw her husband, Brad, on the opposite side of the street rounding the corner of the intersection. She was about to call out and wave when she noticed that he was not alone. His arm was firmly wrapped around a young, attractive woman she had never seen before, although it quickly became evident that they were on familiar terms. Before Marcia could collect her thoughts, they both walked into the front lobby of a large three-star hotel and convention center. Marcia stutter-stepped across the street, eyes unblinking as several surprised drivers slammed on the brakes and honked their horns. As she approached the lobby doors, Marcia could see her husband and his companion laughing together at the front desk. The attendant handed her husband a key. Unable to watch any more, Marcia turned on her heel, fled back to the car and somehow managed to drive herself home, numbly viewing the road through a veil of tears. As she now paces the living room floor, talking with Chris, she fantasizes easily about what she wishes she had done, marching through the crowded lobby, roaring out his name, slapping her across the face, demanding to know what they were doing together. But, then, she is pulled up short by doubt and hesitation. Was Brad attending some conference or convention she had forgotten about? The truth is she did not always pay close attention to his conversations about work. Maybe the woman was simply an out-of-town friend he had not seen in awhile? They had only been married for 18 months; Marcia did not know all of his old acquaintances.

One thing was clear. Regardless of the details, regardless of what she eventually decided to do, Marcia was livid with jealousy, jealousy and suspicion. And this further complicated the tangle of questions unravelling in Marcia's mind, for she was surprised at the raw power of her emotional reaction. It was seemingly beyond her control, which was all the more surprising since she had always thought of herself as a very accepting, broad-minded person, the last person in the world, in fact, who would ever be bothered by something as petty as jealousy. She had been taught that jealousy was a sign of emotional immaturity, but now all she could think was that if this were the case, then she was ready for developmental preschool. Her broad-mindedness had narrowed considerably in very short order. She had to learn the truth, yet she was terrified at the possibility that her suspicions might be confirmed. She had seen her husband being intimate—laughing, talking, sharing, leaning closely against the wind—with someone else. The image of Brad with his arm around another woman was etched indelibly in her memory, and its dark imprint had for the moment banished all peace from her life.

Shakespeare had good reason to describe jealousy as a "green eyed monster," "a poisonous mineral" that gnaws away at our insides.[1] He was simply reporting human experience. As a man with his own troubled marriage, he may even have been reflecting upon his own inner turmoil. Though experts may argue about the psychological causes and social acceptability of jealousy, to the averge lay-person struggling to negotiate long-term, intimate relationships, jealousy is the obvious chaperone of any true romance. Like a love-lorn Jekyll and Hyde, romantic interest spawns a darker alter-ego many find difficult, if not impossible, to control. As psychologist Ayala Pines puts it, jealousy is the shadow side of love.[2]

Given everything that we have learned thus far about the relational nature of the biblical God, particularly God's desire to have an intimate, personal relationship with each of us, it ought to come as no surprise to learn that jealousy may also be a part of the divine personality profile. For example, Yahweh sought to establish an exclusive, covenantal relationship with the people of Israel by saying:

> You shall not make an idol in the form of anything…You shall not worship them…for I, the Lord your God, am a jealous God…
> (Exodus 20:5)

Divine love longs for exclusivity, like a newlywed surprised to find a stranger in the honeymoon suite. Yahweh clearly owns up to a jealous impulse ignited by the covenant people. The question for us is, how are we to conceive of such shadows, such emotionally dark recesses lurking within the divine nature? Is this a God with whom we want to be alone?

God is a jealous God. Whether or not those words strike us as shocking, off-putting, primitive or merely pedestrian will, at least in part, be a function of how we have experienced and then processed jealousy in our own personal lives. For some, the thought of jealousy conjures up memories of long-lost, idyllic love. For others, it reminds us of heart-ache and betrayal. Still others may recall an unhealthy obsession best forgotten. Different histories create different shades of meaning, and our differing intuitions may well incite widely varying responses to the same overture.

John Hinkley was so intensely jealous of Jodie Foster that he not only stalked her but shot the president of the United States in a delusional attempt to win her affections. This is what can happen when the green-eyed monster identifies its prey. Many of us probably believe that jealousy of any sort, whether delusional or not, is an unhealthy sign of emotional instability, a symptom of selfish, petty, possessiveness. So, how am I to respond to the statement that God is a jealous God, especially when God does not say it just once or twice, but repeats it emphatically over and over again? The Old Testament compares God to a jealous lover over 30 times, and more often than not the object of this jealousy (Israel) was less than thrilled by all the attention. Are you and I another Jodie Foster stalked by a divine John Hinkley? Is God a cosmic psychopath threatening to unleash an uninvited attack on my life? Or, perhaps, a petulant child stomping a cosmic foot in a divine temper tantrum? Is such divine jealousy another piece of evidence for the primitive, under-developed nature of Old Testament religion, something to be gratefully transcended by a more civilized devotion? Or might there be a useful lesson here about the potential depths of interpersonal connection available to anyone willing to explore the contours of eternal jealousy? You have probably already guessed the solution I will eventually want to suggest. Let's begin by tackling these questions together.

EXPLORING THE ROOTS OF JEALOUSY

The biblical vocabulary for jealousy is quite consistent throughout both the Old and New Testaments. In fact, there is even a linguistic footprint left in our own language in the form of the word "zeal." This English word is derived from the Greek word *zelos* which is consistently used to translate the Hebrew word *qannā'*, a word that also typically means jealousy.[3] Actually, both *zelos* and *qannā'* can refer more broadly to a condition we might call enthusiasm. To be zealous is to be enthusiastic; whether such enthusiasm is a good thing or a bad thing depends entirely upon its object. For example, if I am enthusiastic in my quest for spiritual well-being, then I am filled with a zeal for God. If, on the other hand, I am enthusiastic about acquiring a new car that you have but I don't, then I am filled with envy for your car. However, if I am enthusiastic about maintaining a valuable relationship that someone else is threatening to destroy, then I am filled with jealousy for my loved one. Zeal, envy and jealousy are all kissin' cousins on the emotional homestead. Each of them may translate the same Greek or Hebrew word because they all arise from the same root: passion. The question is, at the end of the day, what am I passionate about? If jealousy is the back side of love, then envy is the store-front of acquisitiveness. To modify Forrest Gump only slightly, passion is as passion does. The direction in which we aim our desires, and how we then load ourselves up in pursuit of the selected target, makes all the difference in whether our behavior is noble or perverse. Are we selflessly guarding a treasure with our lives or selfishly stealing what rightly belongs to another? We can be equally zealous in either attempt. Context is everything.

However, the particular emotional turmoil that sets jealousy apart requires the introduction of a third party into the equation, further complicating the discussion. Jealousy is typically defined as the protective reaction to some perceived threat to a valued relationship.[4] Jealousy, unlike envy, requires a partner. Envy is like disco; you can do it all alone. Jealousy is like the tango; it takes two.

In our earlier example, Marcia fears that the beautiful stranger wrapped around her husband is an intruder inserting herself where she has no business being, thereby threatening the bond of marital trust that binds Marcia and Brad together. This makes the curvaceous blond a trespasser; and in Marcia's mind every marriage carries with it a large, neon sign brightly flashing "trespassers beware." Before they were married, Marcia knew that she had numerous rivals.[5] Brad was handsome, popular, financially secure and very available. In the early days of their dating relationship, she experienced momentary flashes of jealousy aroused by the other women he dated, but since there was as yet no agreement to exclusivity between them, and she could sense that her interest in Brad was growing more quickly than his interest in her, she knew that it would be inappropriate to openly express her occasional glimpses of the green-eyed monster. In fact, had she done so Brad may well have interpreted her unwelcomed possessiveness as a sign of emotional instability and ended their relationship. However, Marcia was a healthy, secure woman who knew full well the significant value that she alone brought to their relationship, so it was not terribly difficult for her to confront the jealousy elicited by her rivals and dismiss it as understandable but unwarranted.

Eventually, Brad's level of interest began to catch up with her own and she pulled ahead of the pack, so to speak. When Brad finally proposed marriage and they later publicly vowed to remain faithful to each other for the rest of their lives, many of Marcia's former rivals were seated in the audience wiping away their tears. However, their relationships were now permanently altered. The other women would never be rivals again. From now on, any former rival who wanted to take up the old competition with Marcia would become a trespasser. Rivalry was fair play. Trespassing was illegal. Marcia would not feel the least bit embarrassed or constrained about sending a warning shot across the bow of anyone trying to make a pass at her husband, neither could Brad accuse her of emotional immaturity when she scowled at a flirt. They had freely exchanged vows. Promises had been made. There is nothing irrational about wanting to protect the love of your life from outside invasion. Of course, Brad may still want to discuss whether Marcia's jealousy is rational or warranted; he may protest that it is neither, and there may well be plenty of room for discussion or even counselling, but potential jealousy is now a legitimate concern simply because there is a real relationship at stake. How the emotional connections between the two members of the relationship and the perceived trespasser are triangulated may become extremely complicated. Not everyone may see the situation in exactly the same way. Is the jealousy justified? Do both partners understand their relational boundaries in the same way? Has jealousy become only a mechanism for maintaining the other's interest? Are personal insecurities fostering irrational delusions? Does the partner who feels threatened respond obsessively or, worse yet, violently? Can both partners agree upon a solution?

For anyone who has ever personally negotiated jealousy's troubled terrain, you know that the trek can be difficult; and unfortunately, the journey does not always arrive at a safe haven. Consequently, what could appear more daunting than the confrontation of a jealous God? What kind of green-eyed monster must lurk within the one who announces from heaven, "The Lord, whose name is Jealous, is a jealous God" (Exodus 34:14)? However, before tackling this question, let me ask for just one more brief delay. For we first need to understand how our approach to the psychological questions concerning jealousy in human relationships may easily cause us to prejudge the religious questions raised by the claims of God's jealousy for us. And just to make sure that we are aware of our own prejudices and presuppositions on this score, let me offer an oh-so brief survey of modern, psychological research on the complicated emotion we call jealousy. Whether or not we have ever read this kind of material, we all have inhaled at least a few of these notions from the cultural atmosphere around us.

DISSECTING THE MONSTER

It has been estimated that up to 20% of all murders involve a jealous lover, and two-thirds of the women seeking refuge in shelters for battered wives attribute their husband's violence to excessive or unwarranted jealousy. Furthermore, in a nation-wide survey of marriage counselors, jealousy was cited as the major issue in 33% of all client couples under age 50. Yet, clinical psychologists readily admit that, for whatever reasons, surprisingly little empirical research has been done on the subject of jealousy.[6] However, the absence of research has not stopped the theorizing and the broadcasting throughout popular culture of competing attitudes towards jealousy.

The personal evaluation that we each attach to the problem of jealousy will have a great deal to do with our upbringing, including both the time-frame and the social environment in which we were raised.[7] During the *Leave It to Beaver* era of the 1950s and early 60s, jealousy was popularly thought to be a positive, natural expression of love and devotion, in spite of the fact that academia had long been at work laying a foundation for a very contrary attitude. With the rise of sexual experimentation and the alternative lifestyles of the Woodstock generation in the 60s and early 70s, the negative views of jealousy that had been fermenting for some time among Western intellectuals finally found fertile soil. Jealousy was now increasingly associated with the destructive, undermining forces of guilt and poor self-esteem; something to be rejected at all costs. However, by the late 80s through the 90s jealousy was being rehabilitated as our society began reconsidering the benefits of monogamy and fidelity in relationships. To offer just one contemporary example, the most recent, popular study of jealousy, by the evolutionary psychologist David Buss, argues quite strongly that jealousy is an essential ingredient to our survival as a species:[8]

> Jealousy makes people examine their relationships...It teaches couples not to take each other for granted...ensures that they continue to value each other and... indicates that people value the love relationship it protects.

However, migrating from the positive evaluations of jealousy in the 1950s back to the reaffirmations of the 90s was a long, circuitous journey. Major voices in the past had spoken out quite loudly against the social and inter-personal value of jealousy, convincing much of the public that it is something for which any healthy person ought to be ashamed and embarrassed. Two figures, in particular, were especially successful in planting the seeds that now cause many of us to feel uncomfortably self-conscious about our jealousy without knowing why. Those two voices came from opposite sides of the Atlantic, but their influence converged in shaping a powerful social consensus. The speakers were Sigmund Freud and Margaret Mead.

Sigmund Freud, the father of modern psychoanalysis, maintained that although jealousy was a normal, universal human experience, it was also innately pathological.[9] Being jealous was like catching a cold: it happens to everyone, but you are better off without it. Freud identified three different types of jealousy rooted in the complex interactions of three distinct psychological issues. First, "normal jealousy" emerges when something stirs up our unconscious, repressed memories of the Oedipus/Electra complex characteristic of every childhood. According to Freud, all children are naturally jealous for their opposite-sex parent (like the figures Oedipus and Electra of Greek mythology) and secretly wish to eliminate their parental competition. Eventually, normal children experience enough guilt to repress the hostile feelings directed against their same-sex parent, only to have this hostility later reemerge in adulthood in the form of romantic jealousy. Thus jealousy is the reliving of our unresolved, sexual desires for one of our parents—not something to be warmly embraced.

Second, "projected jealousy" is a form of self-deception used to avoid one's own adulterous urges. Again, jealousy masks the guilt you and I subconsciously feel over our own secret desires to be unfaithful; consequently, jealousy is projected as an emotional decoy in order to distract attention away from the real issue. By painting our partner as the one guilty of emotional faithlessness, we avoid our own guilty, inner conflicts.

Third, Freud's "delusional jealousy" is an expression of latent homosexuality. Rather than admit one's own attraction to a member of the same sex, jealousy becomes a way of repressing our sexual excitement by accusing our partner of being interested in the object of our own desire. Jealousy is a psychological trick that those who are confused about their sexual identity play upon themselves in order to remain in the proverbial closet.

It is not difficult to see that, whether the reader agrees with Freud or his swelling ranks of modern-day critics, he clearly paved the way for a universally negative appraisal of any and all jealousy.[10] Popularized versions of Freud's theories, spread through books, magazine articles and hit movies such as *The Snake Pit* (1948), all cast jealousy as the boogie-man that haunted only emotional cripples; to publically admit feelings of jealousy was like confessing that you enjoyed tearing the wings off flies. For example, in 1947 Dr. Boris Sokoloff published an easy to read series of case-studies entitled *Jealousy: A Psychiatric Study* popularizing Freud's views. In dramatic, flowing prose Sokoloff described instance after instance where he had treated jealousy as a serious mental illness in need of psychiatric attention; the good doctor argued that jealousy was an "inbred weakness," "a mental illness," and "a fundamental problem of maladjustment."[11] He concluded his work with this diatribe:[12]

> Love is not responsible for the irrationalities of jealous emotion...true love prevents the excesses of jealousy...An individual whose relationship to the outside world is healthy, who loves others, and who is motivated by positive impulses, is almost unable to be jealous.

The second major voice who succeeded in consigning jealousy to the 20th century netherworld of stunted emotional growth was the anthropologist Margaret Mead. Dr. Mead burst onto the American scene with the publication of her doctoral research in the book *Coming of Age in Samoa* (1928), the best selling anthropological book of all time. Published with the subtitle, *A Psychological Study of Primitive Youth for Western Civilisation*, Mead's work claimed to describe the relaxed attitudes and promiscuous sexual behaviors of an idyllic, Samoan island culture where sexual experimentation was openly encouraged and jealousy was nonexistent. As a committed advocate of cultural determinism—that is, the view that human behavior is shaped entirely by social pressure as opposed to innate, natural tendencies—Mead spent the rest of her life arguing that jealousy was an unnatural, artificial product of restrictive social expectations that bound us in an emotional straight jacket. The quicker we rejected it, the healthier we all would be. From the 1930s throughout the 60s Margaret Mead remained a highly visible public figure who became one of the most effective popularizers of modern social theory. A familiar commentator on radio and television, she contributed a monthly column to the best-selling woman's magazine *Redbook* which offered her a national platform from which she could broadcast her views on human sexuality, views that included the condemnation of jealousy as an "essentially egoistic and selfish" barometer of a lover's insecurity.[13] However, it is equally important to note that she was not always popular with the actual subjects of her study. Native Samoans regularly protested her work as a complete misrepresentation of their culture, and today Mead's Samoan research has been thoroughly discredited as "the result of a prankish hoax" played upon her by the young women she naively interviewed while still an inexperienced doctoral student.[14]

None of us are raised in a vacuum. We all quietly absorb the unstated attitudes of our surrounding culture without ever being clearly told where those assumptions come from or why they are so powerful. Many of us grew up in a society where the whispering intonations of Freud, Mead and others of their ilk quietly, yet pervasively, wooed us with their siren-song, telling us that we should both feel shame over our jealousy and criticize the jealousy of others as unhealthy and unnatural. However, today these attitudes represent a bygone era. Current research is accumulating a wealth of information pointing in exactly the opposite direction. Without doubt, jealousy can become unhealthy; it can be obsessive and even delusional. But in those instances, jealousy itself is not the culprit; it is merely symptomatic of a deeper problem.[15] Jealousy *per se* is no longer to be shunned but is increasingly embraced as a natural, healthy feature of true love. In fact, some psychologists have even begun to speak about problems of "pathological tolerance," which is *the absence of jealousy* when one would normally expect to find it.[16] In other words, the failure to become jealous when an interloper tries to invade our primary love relationship may now be interpreted by some psychologists as a signal of deep, emotional disturbance.

What are we to make of all this?

Let's return to Marcia and Brad for a moment. Hopefully, at some point in their phone conversation, Chris will be able to encourage Marcia to stop maligning herself for feeling emotionally hijacked by the jealousy she is experiencing. The green-eyed monster is not an indication of poor self-esteem, narrow-mindedness, or emotional immaturity. Quite the opposite. What Marcia is feeling is actually a green-eyed watch dog intent upon guarding the inner sanctum of her private garden where she and she alone is free to walk arm-in-arm with her husband. Actually, it would be quite unnatural for Marcia not to feel jealous in this situation. Granted, she will definitely need to keep a close eye upon the ways she chooses to express her jealousy in the future. Buying a gun, haunting the hotel lobby or stalking the strange blond around town would not be wise decisions. The best thing she can do is to own her jealousy as a legitimate emotion, express her pain openly to her husband when he gets home that evening, reassert her rightful (yes, rightful) expectation of fidelity in their marriage, and candidly ask what he was doing with this other woman. That would be the start of a healthy conversation. Depending upon Brad's answers, Marcia can then assess whatever emotions arise next (relief? shock? confusion?) and decide what to do with her lingering jealousy (put it to rest as no longer necessary? or learn to manage it so that it will not get out of control in future conversations?). One thing she never needs to do is feel embarrassed or inadequate for experiencing jealousy towards a trespasser. The green-eyed guard dog was only doing its job.

DOES GOD NEED TO SEE A THERAPIST?

Of course, it is one thing to accept jealousy as a natural part of human relationships. It is quite another to view jealousy as a healthy, normal ingredient in a personal relationship with God. But having now established that any suspicions we hold about the propriety of jealousy should be seriously reexamined, perhaps we can suspend judgment a bit longer as I suggest that we at least give this jealous God the benefit of the doubt. We have already seen that, first and foremost, the Bible describes God as a passionate lover of humanity who invests all of eternity's energy into pursuing a successful, intimate relationship with each of us. Knowing this much basic information about our Creator certainly sets the stage for a religious drama in which God could possibly be subject to jealousy like any other lover who finds her beloved in someone else's tender embrace. Of course, we are still speaking metaphorically about God, as we must with all description of divine emotions. So, as we saw in a previous chapter, we need to remember that using the jealousy metaphor points to both similarity and dissimilarity between God's experience and our own. In other words, as Tertullian would want to remind us, God is both like us and unlike us to the degree that we, the divine image bearers, are both like and unlike God. The important point is not that God experiences jealousy like us, but that we experience jealousy like God—with a twist. When our jealousy is expressed in a healthy fashion, we are reflecting the beauty of the divine life deposited within us, yearning for the security of an unshakeable faithfulness that can withstand all the corrosive tests of time and temptation. On the other hand, whenever human jealousy takes a twisted, unnatural turn (as with abusive husbands and stalkers like John Hinkley), we are contorting God's image to our own evil purposes making a mockery of divine passion and behaving in a most un-godlike manner.

Keeping this metaphorical model in mind, I think I may have a useful way to shine some light on our subject by submitting God to clinical analysis, so to speak. Just for the sake of argument, let's temporarily allow God to be jealous. What might it be like for God to accompany us to a counselor's office, like any other jealous partner in a relationship, where we could talk through our conflicts and discover some useful solutions? To direct this experiment, I have chosen one of the approaches to clinical, jealousy management suggested by Dr. Gregroy White and Dr. Paul Mullen in their book, *Jealousy: Theory, Research and Clinical Strategies.*[17] If we draw upon the biblical material describing God's jealousy and then apply a standard therapeutic method to God's attitude towards us, what sort of conclusions might we draw? Is God's jealousy normal or pathological? Can we find an agreeable solution? In order to address these questions, the doctors' suggested strategy for jealousy management demands that we explore three levels of interaction:

First, the situation that has provoked the jealousy must be identified, then the responsible partner and the trespasser must address their responsibilty to minimize any threat to the jealous partner.

Second, the elements within the relationship that are feeding the jealousy need to be exposed, then both partners must clarify the rules of the relationship to which they will commit themselves.

Third, the therapist must help to uncover the individual characteristics, such as the feelings, behaviors and assumptions of both the jealous subject and the partner, that have generated the jealousy and kept it alive.

As these three levels are traversed the jealousy becomes less and less a mysterious monster, attacking and disappearing at will, and more and more a muzzled animal on a leash, to be walked, caged or released as the couple together decide their future.

HOW IS GOD'S JEALOUSY PROVOKED?

We all have a tendency to see our own jealousy as entirely justified while the other's jealousy is the baseless product of some personality defect. But any good marriage counselor will remind us that this is hardly fair; jealousy arises from a complex interaction of give-and-take where both parties have a stake in the relationship. Thus it is only fitting that a discussion of divine jealousy should eventually lead to a comparison with marriage, for it is the most commonly used biblical metaphor depicting God's passionate love for people. If we are unfamiliar with the Bible, this can sometimes make for strange reading because the writers do not hesitate to explore the boundaries of even the most intimate allusions to male-female relations. The Old Testament prophets frequently refer to Israel, both men and women alike, as God's bride. Sexual intercourse becomes a climactic expression of the mutual surrender God hopes to find with us. Once, the New Testament writer Paul refers to his own jealousy on God's behalf for the church in the Greek city of Corinth, stirred up by their faithlessness to their "husband" Christ (II Corinthians 11:2). Disregard for God, apathy for our relationship, is often described as adultery; it is what happens whenever we direct our spiritual energies towards something or someone else besides the Creator. In fact, the entire Old Testament book of Hosea is built around the imagery of God-the-jilted-cuckold desperately pursuing the young wife who spurns her devoted husband for other lovers.

One of the more elaborate of these unhappy portraits is painted by the Old Testament prophet, Ezekiel. In Ezekiel chapter 16, the writer offers a detailed allegory of the limitless self-sacrifice God willingly extends to each of us. Israel is compared to an unwanted newborn abandoned along the side of the road, still wet with amniotic fluid, naked against the elements, numbed with exhaustion, too weak to cry. The Lord finds this infant no one else wanted and holds the tiny, ugly bag of wrinkled skin and brittle bones with the tender strength found only in the divine arms. God sees the inner beauty

GOD AS JEALOUS LOVER

no one else could discern, the distinctive imprint that was only an oddity to lesser eyes. And so, God nurses the orphan, showering her with undivided attention, meeting her every need, ensuring that the child becomes a healthy, young girl, and the girl grows into a strong, noble woman who has never lacked for anything, either material or emotional. She has always known that she was loved as the apple of the Master's eye, and that he would have given anything, including his life, to see that she was cared for properly.

Eventually, when she comes of age, the Master asks if she would become his bride. (A very permissible step to take in the ancient world). Having kept himself for her all these years, he now invites her to find another, if she prefers, or to accept him, if she will. Her decision is free and uncoerced; she enthusiastically confesses that this has been her childhood dream, just as it has been his mature longing. They unite in marriage and happily pledge themselves to a lifetime of faithfulness. God's heart is given away in the manner of a love-sick school boy who rushes in where angels fear to tread. At that moment, the Creator becomes subject to the possibility of disappointment. The eventuality of rejection is as probable for God as for any other partner in a relationship with a feckless human being. No one stands up before family and friends to take the marriage vow in eager expectation of one day meeting someone else more attractive, more exciting, more desirable. Yet, the tragedy of such broken promises occurs every day in our divorce courts. It does not take long for God's heart to break:

> "I gave you my solemn oath and entered into a covenant with you," declares the Sovereign Lord... "But you lavished your favors on anyone who passed by...You prefer strangers to your own husband!" (Ezekiel 16:8, 15, 32)

Here is the situation provoking heaven's jealousy. God gives us absolutely everything of any value in our lives: life, breath, intellect, vision, imagination, career, family, friends, the morning sunrise, each harvest moon, a large-mouth bass chomping on a treble hook, a dew drop on the pointed petal of a yellow daisy; in fact, anything that expands our life and makes it worth living is given to us by the love of God. That same Creator then asks that we return this love in faith and gratitude, daily acknowledging our dependence. But we have a very hard time doing this. We more easily assert our independence and pretend to have created our success all by ourselves. We grasp ahold of what has been given to us and complain that it is not enough, being quicker to complain that the glass is 1/100s empty than we are to recognize that it is 99/100s full. We kneel at the altar of materialism, bow towards Wall Street, memorize the sacred text of the Dow Jones, and seldom if ever give God more than a second thought each day.

Few of us actually reject God outright like Nietzche (who said God was dead) or Freud (who believed Old Testament religion was at the root of most neurosis), but we do tend to prefer our own personalized substitutes. After all, they are easier to understand. And materialism is only one of the options. Equally eager contenders might take the shape of sex, education, food, career, you name it. Some are even returning to the old, primitive religions. I once had an acquaintance in college who literally molded her own goddess in art class; placing the idol in her dorm room, with incense and candles on either side, she bowed and prayed before it twice each day. Although most of us may never go that far in (literally) shaping our own handmade god, the self-described neo-pagan movement is alive and well (just check the internet), whether it takes the form of praying to the mother-earth goddess Gaia or invoking the animistic spirits of New Age Wicca. Whether the religion is ethereal or down-and-dirty, temporal or eternal, advanced or primitive, technologically driven or purely introspective, the God of the Bible jealously views all such practices as an abandonment of our Creator. We have been asked to recognize that Yahweh and only Yahweh, the God to whom Jesus of Nazareth offered his own daily prayers, is the One to whom we owe our existence and pledge our allegiance. Failure to do this, as far as the biblical God is concerned, is the spiritual equivalent of crawling into bed with a stranger on your honeymoon night.

WHAT GIVES GOD THE RIGHT?

But here comes the rub. Now that we have a better understanding of what it is that provokes God's jealousy, for many of us God's attitude seems thoroughly inappropriate. If we were really sitting in a therapist's office, we would hope to hear the counselor take God down a notch for imposing such outlandish expectations without our consent. No wonder our relationship is not working. Thankfully, this second phase of jealousy management requires us to define the rules of our relationship and identify those elements responsible for the jealousy. In this instance, that seems fairly easy. God is overly possessive, imposing rules of spiritual monogamy to which we never agreed. By any textbook definition, this would seem to put God's jealousy squarely in the pathological category.

Perhaps, at this point, we ought to make room for a distinction between two different types of people. On the one hand, there are those spiritual enquirers who are still in the dating phase of their search for God; that is, they are investigating the options but have stopped short of making any commitments. On the other hand, there are those who would readily admit to a committed, spiritual relationship with the biblical God. At some point in life, these people had taken a step of faith confessing that they had found the God for whom they were searching. Significantly, the Old and New Testaments only apply the jealousy metaphor to this second group: those who claim to know and to love Yahweh, the God of Jesus Christ. God is only explicitly said to become jealous when these people neglect that relationship in a search for new, spiritual alternatives. To folks in this category, God vehemently rejects any interest in such an open marriage and insists upon religious monogamy. In fact, in an almost shockingly extremest turn of the Old Testament metaphor, God occasionally describes attempts to reengage wandering Israel's interest by "flirting" with outsiders, which in this case are the various Gentile nations surrounding Israel:

> Israel has made me jealous with their idols, which are really not gods at all. So now I will make them jealous by giving my affections to the Gentile nations of the world. (Deuteronomy 32:21)

Though this development of the imagery makes many theologians uncomfortable (so that it is once again quickly swept under the convenient rug of anthropomorphism), such passages clearly state that God is not above a bit of heavenly tit-for-tat, if it will motivate Israel's return. In fact, the New Testament taps into this strain of Old Testament tradition in order to explain the rapid expansion of the originally Jewish-Christian movement into the predominantly Gentile, Greco-Roman world (Romans 10:19; 11:11, 14).

Of course, the difference between God and the average lover—an essential distinction that saves God from being a cheat and a cad when making this move—is that God is able to love indiscriminately while remaining perfectly faithful to all the individual recipients of that love. Loving Gentiles does not make God unfaithful to Israel; something for which I, a Gentile, am very grateful. I once heard the story of a man being prosecuted for bigamy whose lawyer tried this defense: his client was compared to a free-wheeling honey bee who was constitutionally obligated to pollinate as many female flowers as possible. I was glad to hear that the jury did not fall for the imagery and that Mr. Honey Bee was convicted of bigamy and sentenced to the maximum penalty allowed. Here is one more way in which God and divine jealousy are not like our human experience with personal relationships. God does not commit bigamy when trying to love as many partners as possible. The Creator loves every creature[18] and yearns for a relationship with each and every one of us.[19]

We have bumped up against another of those prickly limitations of the biblical metaphor. God is like us in becoming jealous over covenant partners who wander. But God is unlike us in possessing the ability to extend that love far beyond the boundaries of the covenant without cheating. We are untangling the intersection of two different, yet related, metaphors for the relationship between God and people: one is God as marriage partner, the other is God as creator. The marriage partner who begins cruising singles' bars in an effort to reignite her husband's romantic interest is foolishly playing with fire. But the artist who is equally passionate about every work she ever produced, whether it sits on her mantle or was sold at auction, is not being foolish; she is only being passionate about her art. When we confront the God who is both our Creator (and is equally passionate about each and every one of us), as well as our eternal Suitor (who wants an intimate place in our lives), we should not be surprised to learn that this type of God is also jealous for those who have never given biblical religion a second thought. This is why it is not pathological for God to feel jealousy over people who have never once turned towards heaven. If I began experiencing intense jealousy over every woman I met, my wife would have good reason to make an appointment for me to see a psychiatrist. My behavior would be entirely irrational. But then, I am not the Creator who lovingly designed and tenderly molded each of those individuals knowing full well they can best function only while enjoying an intimate relationship with me. This is an essential difference between God's jealousy and my own.

Similarly, I cannot look at my wife and know beyond a shadow of a doubt that I am the best man she could have ever married. Her grandmother, for one, believed that she was making a big mistake. But ever since that wedding day in 1976 when I walked the aisle with sweaty palms and a bowling ball in the pit of my stomach, I have every right to drive off any and all would-be trespassers. However, if my bride had unexpectedly said "I don't" instead of "I do", the jealousy I sometimes feel over her would be totally out of line. God, on the other hand, does know beyond any shadow of a doubt that there will never be a better place for us to spend our lives than in the permanent embrace of the divine arms. As our Creator, God has every reason to be jealous for each of us. That is not pathology; that is the pathos of a God who unconditionally loves every one of us, regardless of whether or not we ever return that love.

DOES GOD NEED HEALTHIER SELF-ESTEEM?

Step three in our therapy session requires us to focus upon the individual characteristics of the jealous party including the feelings and behaviors associated with that jealousy. Traditionally, low self-esteem was believed to be the principle, motivating force behind all jealousy. It was thought to be a symptom of personal insecurity eating away at a relationship. However, more recent studies have been unable to find support for this older assumption, and many appear to undermine it altogether.[20] Jealousy and self-esteem are like the proverbial chicken-and-egg conundrum; it is impossible to determine which comes first. Perhaps low self-esteem (if it exists) is the result, not the cause, of whatever situation created the jealousy?[21] I know that I would certainly develop some deep insecurities if my wife suddenly announced that she was leaving me for some young stud. In any event, a broad survey of current research reveals a number of other characteristics that seem to accompany jealousy more predictably. For instance, jealousy is most likely to be stronger in the partner who:[22]

- has the greater commitment to faithful monogamy
- places the higher value and makes the greater investment in the relationship
- feels him/herself to be the weaker more dependant member
- believes him/herself to be the partner less likely to find a new relationship

None of these characteristics are surprising when we remember that jealousy is defined as a reaction to a perceived threat to a valued relationship. It makes sense that if either party felt more vulnerable to outside threats, that this would also be the member more likely to experience jealousy as a defensive maneuver. For those of us with some traditional religious sensibility, it does not seem incongruous to continue our imaginary counseling session by applying the first two categories of personality traits to the jealous God found in the Bible. After all, this is the God of holy love, the God who IS love who freely offers unshakeable, never-ending devotion to you and me before ever being asked or approached. In fact, the absence of jealousy ought to raise our suspicions. If God were never jealous, we would have every reason to question the sincerity of these purported pledges to commitment. The absence of jealousy is a sign of indifference; emotional indifference or emotional disturbance, take your pick.[23] In this respect, God's jealousy provides welcomed reassurance that I am genuinely loved, that God will never let me go, that I will never be unwanted. Because God is jealous, we know that heaven will always ache for our company.

However, what about the third and fourth sets of characteristics? How can our counseling analogy possibly continue once we recognize that the more jealous party is also typically the more dependent, less desirable partner who believes herself less capable of establishing another relationship? How could that conceivably describe God?

GOD AS JEALOUS LOVER

The answer to this question will partly depend upon whether our religious sympathies lie with Clement or Tertullian, Plato or Moses. A God who offers people real freedom to choose, and then respects that freedom by honoring their decisions, might well wonder about the likelihood of any future relationships given the tenuous fabric of human devotion. This is the kind of God who asks "what if" questions (see chapter 3), and wonders aloud, "What more can I do to get my people's attention?" (see Hosea 6:4), and can actually be surprised at human stubbornness (Jeremiah 3:7). A God of restraint is willingly dependent upon human response, waiting for the creature to indicate the Creator's next available move. By becoming humanity's servant, God adopts the weaker position, the position that most readily explains divine jealousy. The fact is, God does invest more into our relationship. God pledges never to leave us, but we are free to walk away at any time—and often do. This Old Testament tradition continues into the New Testament when Jesus, speaking on God's behalf, says to the crowds agitating for his execution:

> How often I have longed to gather you together, as a hen gathers her chicks under her wings, but you were not willing.
> (Matthew 23:37)

You were not willing. Human willfullness is enough to give God pause and to bring about the renegotiation of the divine will. The dependent God who must patiently wait for the rebellious child to return home in his own time continues to reach out, inviting, never coercing, always intensely jealous, anything but indifferent. This God never forgets to leave the porch light on and the front door unlocked.

This facet of the Old Testament tradition finds ultimate expression, according to Christian belief, in the sacrificial death of Jesus Christ on the cross. Jesus describes his crucifixion as the final depiction of the extreme measures God was willing to take in remaining the One who demonstrates strength by means of the most abject weakness. To the very end, God works most powerfully to convince us while resolutely refusing to coerce us. Consequently, Jesus says:

> I did not come to be served but to serve, and to give my life as a ransom for many. (Mark 10:45)

The cross holding aloft the crucified God has always been the impediment upon which even the most determined Christian Platonists, like Clement of Alexandria and Origen, have consistently run aground. Origen, we recall, was Clement's brilliant successor heading up the Christian, philosophical academy at Alexandria. In his theological works, he was every bit as devoted to Plato's philosophy as was his famous predecessor. Origen also regularly described God as impassible, free of all emotion, immune to any change, and eternally beyond the influence of human beings. However, as often seems to happen, the philosophical rigour applied in writing a theological treatise tends to melt, if not evaporate altogether, when it comes time to preach and teach from the Bible itself. The most telling example of this metamorphosis is found in a series of homilies (short messages) given by Origen on the Old Testament prophet, Ezekiel. When it came time for Origen to comment on chapter 16, the realities of biblical language overwhelmed apparent, philosophical necessity. The Platonist was consumed by the Biblicist. Ezekiel's comparison of God to the doting suitor who suffers the rejection of his beloved leads Origen into a moving digression on the Christian doctrine of the incarnation: that is, God's decision to become a human being in order to die for us on the cross:[24]

> He (sic) descended to earth in pity for the human race. He suffered our sufferings, before he suffered the cross and condescended to take our flesh upon himself. For if he had not suffered, he would not have come to take part in human life. First he suffers, then he descends and is seen. What is the emotion that he suffers for us? It is the emotion of love...The Father himself is not impassible...He suffers something of love and comes to be in a situation where, because of the greatness of his nature, he cannot be; and for our sake he experiences human emotion.

God deliberately enters into a situation where, due to "the greatness" of the divine nature, the Creator logically "cannot be" and, yet, very clearly is. In this statement, Origen echoes Tertullian's famous rejoinder that the death of God in Christ "is certain because it is impossible" (see chapter one). The Author of virility surrenders to impotence. Ultimate strength melts into final weakness. The Master yields all control. The Creator is extinguished by the creation. Eternal life dies. Through the power of sacrificial love, eternal jealousy finds a way to turn the weaker more dependent partner into the savior of all future divine-human relationships. God is jealous because God is love. That love does not lead to complaint or to hysteria but to further service and ultimate sacrifice—death on a cross.

AN EPILOGUE

Though she thought her heart would burst in the waiting, Marcia met Brad at the door when he came home that evening. After beginning somewhat defensively, Brad quickly assured his wife that her fears were unfounded. And as the conversation progressed, Marcia became convinced that Brad was telling the truth. While attending a business conference downtown (Marcia filed away a memo to herself: listen more closely when Brad talks about his job), Brad unexpectedly ran into an old girlfriend who had flown in for the same conference. They had lunch together to catch up on old times, and Brad admits that, as a newly-newlywed, he was probably a bit friendlier with his old flame than was appropriate. As they returned to the front desk to learn the revised schedule for that afternoon's sessions, the clerk mistakenly handed her room key to Brad. He blushed; her smile indicated that she was not opposed to his holding onto it. Somewhat flustered, Brad gave her the key and reminded her that he was now a happily married man. She jokingly said, "Rats," as they walked to the adjacent conference room. (Brad thought it best not to tell Marcia about that comment).

Though, at the time, Brad's chance encounter only seemed like an innocent, playful flirtation, seeing his wife's distress now filled him with an odd combination of guilt and elation: guilt because he knew that he had been flirtatious, had sent his friend totally inappropriate signals, and had inadvertently hurt his wife; elation because he was being given a deep and abiding insight into how much he meant to this woman. He was intensely sorry that his behavior had caused her so much pain, but he was also unexpectedly flattered that she would react as she had. It was reassuring to know that Marcia felt this possessive of him; he liked it. No sacrifice was involved in forgoing one night stands with strangers in order to be fully devoted to the one woman who was filled with jealous for him. He wanted to be wanted. With Marcia, he knew that he was.

5

WHEN GOD GROWS TIRED

What Wears God Out?

How wearisome
Eternity so spent in worship paid
To whom we hate.
—John Milton
Paradise Lost, 2.247-249

Brokenness is best experienced vicariously. Reading such classic, romantic tales as *Madame Bovary* or *Anna Karenina*, the stories of two married women who stretch their sexual wings and fly into the arms of men other than their husbands, may provide a poignant catharsis over the lament of lost opportunity, the corrupting power of stolen fruit or the fragility of physical passion, but few of us would ever want to trade places with Mr. Bovary or Mr. Karenina in the real world. A gifted storyteller's ability to conjure up sympathy for the frustrated wanderer easily overpowers our natural tendency to defend the plain, predictable spouse left home alone. It is one thing to read about another's misfortune, quite another to become the subject of the story yourself. Can any cascade of flowing prose, no matter how artfully constructed, dilute the pain a real, flesh and blood person feels when his or her spouse is discovered in someone else's bed?

My years of working in the church have provided many opportunities to hear the stories of men and women who were confronted with that very scene. Listening to their stories was never romantic. For example, I think of a recently divorced friend I will call Bill. Ten years ago his wife ran off with another man only to return home a few weeks later after prince charming had gotten bored with her and vanished into thin air. Bill loved his wife desperately, accepted her back and the two of them began regular counseling together, not just to rebuild what they once had but to create something new and better for them both. Bill describes that decade as the most arduous ten years of his life, made almost impossibly complicated by the fact that his wife was not particularly interested in making the relationship any better. Bill's recent divorce proceeded after getting the green light from his two, adult children. "Dad," they said, "we don't want to see you hurt anymore. Let mom go if that's what she wants." So, he did. He continued to love her as much as he ever had, but she had taken up with yet another man. This time Bill did not even know where she had gone. He is still working through the confusing mailstrom of grief, guilt, shame, anger, jealousy, hatred, rejection, remorse and loneliness that boils within him every single day. Perhaps a novelist could rewrite my friend's story in such a way as to cause the reader to romantically empathize with the wayward wife, to even urge her on in her secret dalliances, but I would kindly suggest that you please not ask Bill to read it.

My friend loved his wife. But in the face of repeated rejection he was forced to make a judgment. In part because of his love, and in part because of his own pain, he determined that it was time to stop fighting and to allow her to finally have her way. She no longer wanted a life with him, with the mundane, repetitious mediocrity of meatloaf dinners, soccer practice, mortgage payments and encroaching, male-pattern baldness. So he let her go, and this time she will not be welcomed back should the latest lothario leave her high and dry at the Holiday Inn.

Sometimes a reluctant judgment to separate is the only thing love is allowed to give. Even the deepest devotion can be worn down by persistent rejection. In fact, there comes a point where the refusal to let go creates its own madness. How many times could we watch my friend vainly search the city's back streets, hoping for a chance encounter with his disinterested wife, before his fierce devotion lost its aura of nobility and degenerated into a pitiful neurosis?

Believe it or not, there also comes a point where the God of the Bible admits to giving up, not because human recalcitrance erodes heaven's love, but because divine love refuses to violate personal freedom. As we saw in chapter three, God is no spiritual rapist. The legendary Hound of Heaven[1] will doggedly pursue us until we decide to stop running and surrender, but it will never sink its teeth into our haunches to bring us down like a terrified deer too exhausted to take another step. God is willing to let us go if we insist, if we run long enough, if we refuse the invitation often enough, if we insist on following our own path loudly enough. In biblical language, God's reluctant decision to abandon the pursuit is called judgment. The basis of divine judgment is not indifference but love, not impatience but the painfully considered decision to finally grant what we demand. The fact that our demands are often self-destructive explains both God's seemingly endless delay before granting them, as well as the grief and misery we typically associate with the notion of the final judgment.

EVEN GOD GETS TIRED

The Old Testament admits that there comes a point where even the Creator grows tired, not from the physical exertion of creating a universe out of nothing, but from the emotional toll exacted by waiting for people who never—never!—keep their appointments. Yahweh says:

> You have forsaken me and turned your backs upon me...I am weary of always giving you another chance. (Jeremiah 15:6)

This passage provides an intriguing combination of images. We have both the language of divine repentance, which we discussed in chapter three, as well as a reference to heavenly exhaustion. God is worn out by the need to be incessantly shifting position in response to human recalcitrance, an ingrained stubbornness less like an immovable object than it is a darting, flitting butterfly eluding every jab of the divine net. We refuse to stand still, no matter how many times we are asked. Eventually, even God admits to exasperation, and it precipitates the expression of final judgment. The result of this heavenly fatigue is God's finally allowing us to have our own way. If a life without God is what we want, then that is the life we will be allowed to have.

In the original historical context, the prophet Jeremiah's warning refers to a particular national tragedy: the people of Israel will be taken captive by the rapacious empire of Babylon. In a series of increasingly severe conquests, the Babylonian king Nebuchadnezzar would eventually scoop up Israel and carry her away into foreign exile across the Euphrates (587 B.C.). In the long run, this too becomes a part of God's strategy to eventually recapture Israel's attention and to demonstrate one more time how futile life becomes apart from a personal relationship with Yahweh. And for one more brief period the reminder works: the people will turn back to their God and find their fortunes restored. Israel is eventually released from exile in 538 B.C., after the Babylonians fall to the Medo-Persian empire—an event the Israelite prophets interpreted as God's providential answer to their prayers for deliverance:

> (The Lord says), "I will raise up Cyrus (the Persian king) in my righteousness:
> He will rebuild my city (Jerusalem)
> and set my exiles free." (Isaiah 45:13)

However, there are other places in the Bible where such specific historical references take on new dimensions, projecting additional layers of significance. A specific, historical complaint may become an image of permanent, future conditions. Consequently, the language of temporary exile can be transformed into a warning about final, universal judgment upon all wickedness. Four more times the Old

Testament prophets warn Israel about the consequences of divine weariness. For example:[2]

> I am weary of bearing your empty formalities.
> When you spread out your hands in prayer,
> I will hide my eyes from you...(Isaiah 1:14-15)

> You have burdened me with your sins;
> and wearied me with your offenses. (Isaiah 43:24)

Such Old Testament warnings of impending judgment upon Israel become the standard paradigm for New Testament warnings about God's eventual judgment upon the entire world. This is not an unusual observation, although it is worth noting that while the New Testament regularly associates such judgment with God's anger (see chapter two), it is never connected with anything like divine weariness (at least, not that I can see). However, this in itself cries out for some explanation since the sheer audacity of an Israelite prophet declaring that divine judgment results from the Creator's exhaustion is nothing short of breathtaking. In fact, there is very early evidence suggesting that some, even within the Jewish community, found this imagery offensive enough to eliminate it when opportunity arose.

By the time the Medo-Persian empire had been rolled back by Alexander the Great (332-323 B.C.), the Greek language had thoroughly replaced Hebrew as the *lingua franca* of the large and influential Jewish community now resident in Egypt. Alexander, a devoted pupil of Aristotle, had zealously promoted Greek culture, language, art and philosophy all throughout his territorial conquests, believing that the Hellenization process could serve as the glue that would bind his growing empire together. The Egyptian capital of Alexandria had also become the intellectual center of the known world housing the largest library ever collected until modern times. By the 3rd century B.C. the Hebrew language was all but dead outside the land of Palestine, and the all pervasive influence of Hellenistic sophistication easily made Judaism appear like a primitive, backwoods religion to the educated readers of Socrates, Plato and Aristotle—or at least, this was the self-conscious fear of the Jewish community. In order to keep their scriptures alive and to demonstrate the continuing relevance of their religion to Hellenistic society, the Jewish leadership initiated a ground breaking project: to translate the Hebrew scriptures into Greek. The result became known as the Septuagint (often abbreviated as the LXX).

As the first translation of the Hebrew Bible, or any other literary work of comparable size, into another language, the Septuagint "marks a milestone in human culture."[3] Without it Philo would have had a much more difficult time insinuating Plato's philosophy into his Old Testament interpretation (see chapter one), and we have already seen the influence his writings had upon the future development of the Christian perspective on God. But an investigation of the Septuagint suggests that Philo may have discovered a subtle invitation to such philosophical reinterpretation within the translation itself. Of particular interest to us is the fact that no translator was able to bring himself to honor the prophets' original intent when translating the passages describing divine weariness; none of them would render the Hebrew literally. Apparently, it was inconceivable that God could ever be described as feeling tired, either literally or symbolically. So the prophet must have meant something else. We can observe the subtle influence of the Hellenistic mindset at work in the various alternatives selected by these ancient translators. In every instance, the original reference to weariness was reconfigured to make it more acceptable.[4]

Furthermore, since the Septuagint was to become the primary version of the Old Testament read by the New Testament writers, it is not surprising to learn that there is no evidence of a divine weariness theme anywhere in the New Testament documents either. As a result, an intriguing aspect of the Old Testament perspective on the divine character and final judgment has been thoroughly neglected; a multifaceted phenomenon was glossed over, in part I suspect, because it was grossly out of step with prevailing philosophical presuppositions. We need to recapture the provocative Old Testament imagery that describes divine judgment as the reaction of a Creator who is simply worn out by the incessant wrangling of rebellious, recalcitrant people.

Earlier we discovered that God's willingness to repent or to have a change of heart appears at the intersection of three divine impulses:

mercy, justice and responsiveness. God is more than ready, willing and able to entertain a redefinition of relationships if and when we are willing to change our behavior. The additional notion that God may also become worn out by our endless chants of "eenee, meenee, minee, mo" reminds us once again to sift through the biblical metaphors carefully. One of the prophets who warns of God's weariness also tells us that:

> The Lord is the everlasting God,
> the Creator of the ends of the earth
> ...who will not grow tired or weary...(Isaiah 40:28)

How does a God incapable of weariness become weary? The simplistic answer is to conclude that the author contradicts himself, but I suggest that we give Isaiah the benefit of the doubt and dig a little deeper.

It was inconceivable for an Old Testament prophet to imagine Yahweh with a physical body. Human beings may tire easily from over exertion (see Isaiah 40:29-31[5]) but not the Creator of the universe. There is no heavenly muscle tissue to feel the burn as cosmic, lactic acid builds up in the divine thighs. The angels never spot for one another during heavenly workouts. God cannot tear a cartilege or pull a groin pushing the limits of divine stamina. In this respect, weariness does not relate to God in quite the same way as anger, jealousy and disappointment. Granted, there may well be physiological responses to these emotions when experienced by a human being (surges of adrenaline or seratonin, an increase in heart rate), but the experiences themselves are not obviously dependant upon possessing a physical body. Just think of how easily our bedtime stories around the campfire revolve around angry spirits and disgruntled spooks. Weariness, however, is intrinsically physical. Exertion and exhaustion go together. In using the term metaphorically, I compare the feeling of physical depletion called weariness to the emotional drain caused by some challenging situation, and I then describe myself as "worn out" (psychologically); perhaps my patience has been "exhausted," so that I have no more "effort" to give. This use of exhaustion language is so commonplace we hardly think of it as metaphorical at all, but it is. Consequently, when the Old Testament prophets describe God as growing weary, we may have a vague, intuitive sense of what is meant, but the precise content remains elusive. The reason for this elusiveness is that we are reading what might be called a metaphor once removed. It is the metaphorical use of a metaphor.

Hopefully, we are now in a position to see that the prophets' weariness language is telling us that not even God's patience is drawn from a bottomless well. Divine love will extend innumerable opportunities for prodigal children to return home, but the front door will not remain open indefinitely. The window of opportunity eventually closes, and the candle in the window will one day be blown out. Thus when the prophet says that God is weary of changing the divine plan, it is a final warning that we were too stubborn for too long. God has not turned away from us; we will be allowed to enjoy the full and lasting consequences of our persistent decision to turn away from God.

DOES GOD EVER GET SICK AND TIRED OF US?

If I had a nickel for every time I heard my mother say, "I am so sick and tired of you kids doing such-and-such," I would be a wealthy man. I do not think I was any more troublesome than an average child, but I must admit that I did love to tease my younger brother and sister. I now know from first hand experience how the incessant racket of bickering children can grate on raw, parental nerves. Though I have tried to keep my childhood oath to never sound like my own parents, I know how they felt, and I must confess to sometimes coming close to speaking in this universal idiom of exasperated parents.

The first time I heard my mother use this phrase, I may have paused and wondered for a moment if she had a fever and wanted to see a doctor. I will never forget the first time I heard my father say that he had to see a man about a horse. Boy, was I excited. However, just as I quickly figured out that my father was not buying me a horse, I also quickly learned that "being sick and tired" did not necessarily mean that my mother was ill or sleepy. Though she may have been physically sick and tired too, that was not the primary import of the phrase. The appropriate response was not for me to dial 911 but to stop causing trouble. She was speaking (or shouting, as the case may be) metaphorically. My mother was comparing her emotional condition (unknown to me) to the physical conditions of illness and exhaustion (with which I was familiar). The point of that comparison was to draw my attention to the emotional reality about to confront my backside if I did not cease and desist from tormenting my brother and sister—namely, the loss of all motherly patience. In other words, a sick and tired mother meant that she would no longer tolerate me giving my brother another dutch rub. Action was about to be taken, action precipitated by my behavior. Maternal mercy had patiently withheld judgment, but the injustice of my teasing, together with my flagrant persistence in ignoring her warnings, meant that the grace period was over. Toleration ended as soon as mom got sick and tired.

At various points throughout this study we have been reminded of Tertullian's wise words when he rooted his argument for the reality of divine emotions in the observation that human beings were created in the image of God. Attributing emotions to God is not an anthropomorphism (metaphorically describing God in human terms); rather, the human emotional response to life is a theomorphism (humanity expressing itself in God-like terms). In other words, we reflect our Creator not vice versa. We have also repeatedly noted that just as every metaphor has its limits, so too any analogy between God and human beings will eventually breakdown not only because of the inherent limits of metaphor, but also because of the huge disparity between perfect divinity and imperfect humanity. To the extent that we continue to reflect God's image, our emotional lives testify to the contours of God's own emotional life. But to the extent that human emotions have been twisted and defaced by such evil as selfishness, greed or lust, then God's emotional life is unlike ours. God knows perfect love, love that is entirely self-giving, never intent upon consuming the other for one's own benefit. God knows perfect jealousy, jealousy that is never tainted by vindictiveness or revenge. God also knows perfect weariness, the weariness of waiting, being stood up and rescheduling, waiting, being stood up and rescheduling, over and over and over again, until you finally face the fact that your date is never going to appear. Perfect weariness is not worn out from holding back anger but from being repeatedly ignored. Perfect weariness does not bark through gritted teeth but resigns itself to reality: the offer of love is never going to be reciprocated. God's pronouncement of final judgment will not be vindictive or spiteful. It will simply be time to acknowledge the facts. Certain of us refuse to listen, refuse to repent, refuse to acknowledge responsibility for wrongdoing, refuse to receive divine forgiveness. Some people just persist in refusing.

My generation grew up watching Charlie Brown get snookered by Lucy every year. Each fall she would bring out a brand new, genuine, hand-stitched pigskin. She invited Charlie Brown out to the park where, promising to hold the football, she urged him to make the first kick of the season. Of course, we already know where this is going. The boy with the big, round head has been here many times before. Like clockwork, Lucy had been pulling the same annual stunt. Pleading with Charlie Brown to take a running start, she invariably pulled the ball away at the last moment, leaving the would-be kicker to fly through the air with no one to catch him. No matter how many people warned him, no matter how many memories of past betrayal raised their ugly heads, hope sprung eternal for the lonely, little boy who wanted to believe that one day Lucy would tell the truth and his trust in her friendship would be vindicated. No one would blame him for eventually deciding that enough is enough. In fact, some of us might have cheered him on if he were to give Lucy a few choice words and kick something besides the ball. Knowing Charlie Brown, however, we can be confident that there would be no anger in his voice, only disappointment that Lucy and he could never share the fun of a game of touch football.

CAN'T GOD FIND ANOTHER WAY?

There was a time when the prospects of eternal judgment were universally accepted by western civilization. With roots going at least as far back as the ancient Egyptians and Babylonians, the belief in a final judgment that would settle the eternal boundaries between reward and punishment has been a commonplace in western religion.⁶ Plato's discussion of the death of Socrates, in the *Phaedo*, muses at length about the afterlife and the final retribution for our behavior in this life. Plato offers a lengthy description of the underworld and the fate awaiting the virtuous and the wicked:⁷

> All those who are thought to be incurable because of the greatness of their sins...are thrown into Tartarus from which they never come out.

The Tartarus was a chasm through the center of the earth in which all the subterranean rivers of punishment and purification flowed. Humanity was graded from the redeemable to the incorrigible and dealt with accordingly as the dead were swept away in the appropriate current of cleansing water or burning flame.

For centuries European men and women conducted their lives in the shadows of inescapable reminders of death's inevitability and the permanence of the afterlife. Works such as Michelangelo's (1475-1564) monstrous *Last Judgment*, covering the nearly 2500 square feet of the altar wall in the Sistine Chapel, provided visual descriptions of the inescapable judgment for a largely illiterate population. Europe was dotted all throughout with such treatments of the subject, and even though none could rival Michelangelo's masterpiece, his work was not unique in its represention of horror for the damned and blessing for the redeemed. Combining images from the New Testament *Apocalypse* with Dante's *Inferno*, Michelangelo depicts a cosmic Christ descending for the final judgment surrounded by his heavenly cohorts. Nearly 400 figures swirl in organized chaos while the great Renaissance artist portrays the resurrection of the sleepy faithful to immortality while wiping death from their eyes. Martyrs are vindicated; the powerful are condemned. Angels and demons are locked in a last ditch tug-of-war over the souls of God's people as Satan makes one final bid to wreck as many as possible. Since the last judgment will expose every secret to the eternal light of God's discernment, from which nothing can hide, the majority of the figures twist, cuddle, tumble and writhe in Herculean nudity—something that provoked accusations of blasphemy in Michelangelo's own day and was quickly remedied by the Vatican's commissioning of assistants to add discreetly folded drapery over some 36 figures considered too provocative for public viewing. The jaws of the underworld, backlit by the inner glow of flames eminating from Hades' catacombs, yawn directly above the head of any priest conducting the Mass, providing a stark reminder of the crucial choices being made by the participants.

Just below the center point of the fresco is a band of angels blowing their trumpets and opening a pair of books. One archangel holds a small book showing its contents to the righteous men and women climbing from their tombs on the left. On the right, two angels are required to hold open a much larger book being displayed to the damned as they are led away by Charon (the boatman of Greek mythology who ferried souls to the underworld) and Minos (the stone-hearted judge of the dead who damned the wicked). Michelangelo's inclusion of these Greek mythological figures supplied his critics with more ammunition to attack his work, but the scene's import is entirely in keeping with the New Testament description of the judgment day. That is, the final judgment is not so much the moment when God makes a decision about our fate as much as it is the moment at which God stops delaying the final consequences of our own choices. Here is the way the New Testament *Apocalypse* describes that moment:

> I saw the dead, great and small, standing before the throne, and (on one side) the books [plural] were opened. And (on the other side) another book [singular] was opened, which is the book of life. The dead were judged according to what they had done as recorded in the books...each person was judged according to what they had done...If anyone's name was not found written in the book of life, they were thrown into the lake of fire. (Revelation 20:12-15)

The ancient, Old Testament imagery of the book of life (singular) depicted the heavenly ledger preserving the names of all those who had responded to God's offer of relationship.[8] In the New Testament, the book of life is not a record of personal performance but a testimony to one's acceptance of the good news of the gospel. On the other hand are the books (plural) recording every decision made and every action taken throughout the entire course of human history—from Adolf Hitler to your sweet aunt Minnie—including each individual decision to ignore the Creator's invitation. The biblical imagery makes it clear that the final judgment is not really God's work but ours. "The choice of heaven or hell is a choice between ultimate union with God and ultimate independence from God."[9] We are given an eternity to enjoy all the benefits of whatever we chose to value in our lifetime. Those who chose to live without God are granted an eternity without God. The angelic display of books simply confirms the justice of God's final separation. Any possible protest can be answered by the eternally preserved record of individual decisions.

Michelangelo's glorified Christ raises his right arm as if literally pulling the righteous from their tombs by invisible cords; he simultaneously peers down to his left gazing at those being led away into Hades. He does not look angry; it is an expression of dispassionate resignation. There is no rage, no piercing stare, no lightning bolt, only the ever-widening gulf of an eternal divide slowly separating the larger portion of humanity from their Creator. I have always been intrigued by Michelango's decision to portray Christ in this way. The focal point for how a viewer would understand God's disposition at this pivotal moment is found in a half-turned face with downcast eyes, neither smiling nor frowning, only watching the inevitable unfold. Michelangelo's instincts were right on target, I believe. Christ arrives at the dock for the ship's departure and then bids farewell as we condemn ourselves to an endless journey away from God.

This awareness of profound loss is the root out of which all the traditional, symbolic foliage of hellacious fire and brimstone, pain and horror grows. Imagine the simultaneous realization of two diametrically opposed insights at precisely the same moment. First, as if a veil were lifted from our eyes, we suddenly find ourselves engulfed by the personal embodiment of complete goodness, overwhelmed by incomparable beauty and riveted by a compelling realization that surrending ourselves to this perfect love would have been the first step towards discovering the essence and meaning of our existence. But, then, having just glimpsed the promised land, a gaping rift opens at our feet separating us from our true destination and the contentment that might have been. Then imagine that those two sensations—the aroma of perfection fueling our grief over its absence on the one hand, and the vacuum of an eternity without God embellishing our dreams about all that ought to have been on the other—imagine those two sensations eternally colliding within the same heart like two, massive bighorn sheep going head to head. That repetitious collision is the fuel for endless, gut-wrenching lament.

Belief in eternal judgment is as rare today as are public displays of Renaissance art. The rationalistic Enlightenment credo—seeing is believing—left little room for such "irrational" beliefs as heaven or hell, although the general public has been slower to surrender its hope in heavenly bliss than its fear of eternal torment.[10] Yet, as the philosopher Jonathan Kvanvig has written, "(T)he only way to avoid the problem of hell is to limit the significance of Christianity to earthly life."[11] Yet, the yearning for a spiritual existence beyond the material limitations of the here and the now is the very hunger that draws many of us to religion in the first place. We want to know if there is something more to life than the immediate failures, or even the partial successes, experienced in this world. And if we cannot finally know, then we at least want to be able to believe. And, if such a future exists, will it finally resolve our unanswered questions? Will it bring justice? Will it effect restitution? Will it right the wrongs and vindicate the oppressed? If an eternal God wants to have an eternal relationship with us, then there must be an eternity somewhere that accomplishes all of these things. This is not just the logic of faith; it is a logic hardwired into our humanity.

IS GOD SMALLER THAN WE THINK OR BIGGER THAN WE IMAGINE?

Naturally, a variety of questions come to mind as soon as we hear the words eternal judgment. As I conclude this chapter, I will try to answer what seem to me to be the three most common objections:

First, how can a God of real love not find some way of rescuing everyone irrespective of the personal decisions they may (or may not) make? An all-powerful, all-loving God ought to do whatever is necessary to spare the beloved. Divine love will always love even those who fail to love in return.

The second objection, closely related to the first, suggests that it is contradictory for an infinite God to lose patience. An infinite God ought to have infinite patience. Explaining that there is no divine body to grow weary does not relieve the exhaustion metaphor of its awkwardness. By definition, a limitless God cannot be impatient.

These two objections may be answered together since they both relate to the difference I am trying to highlight between the God of the philosophers (described by Clement of Alexandria) and the God of biblical revelation (defended by Tertullian). Personal relationship only develops in and through personal revelation. I reveal something of myself to you; you show something new about yourself to me. The more we learn about each other through our mutual exchange, the closer we are drawn together. My theoretical reconstructions of logical possibilities or impossibilities for your life are rendered impotent by the reality of who you actually are. You are what you are not what I might wish you to be. I can imagine whatever I like about you, but my dreams will have no power to shape reality unless you freely choose to respond to my suggestions by changing yourself. This is why I am never particularly impressed by philosophical arguments about what God "ought" to be doing or what is "logically" necessary for the divine. If God is, in fact, a person (yet another metaphor) seeking relationship with me (as the Bible maintains), then it is incumbent upon me to receive whatever God has to reveal just as I would with any other friend in personal conversation.

Yet, this is precisely the point that these two objections fail to grasp. God is not an absolute from which we may logically abstract personal attributes. God is an intimate being who has condescended to interact with us. I vividly remember the first time my doctoral supervisor invited my family over to his home for dinner. My son was 5 years old at the time and not very interested in adult conversation, so my host got out a well-worn, cardboard box full of his son's old model cars and trucks. My very respectable, British mentor then got down on his hands and knees with my little boy and began a series of road races around the living room carpet. I was both amused and taken aback. My immediate response was to protest, to tell him to get up. But it was not my place to object or to insist that such behavior was demeaning. Who was I to tell my professor that he was too well-respected to be playing with toys and little children on the floor? Prior to that moment such a scenario had been inconceivable to me, but then I had not really known my professor very well, had I?

The Bible tells us that God is love. Perfect love "must be willing to suffer even total loss in allowing another to pursue what they most deeply want."[12] My friend Bill exhibited such love when he allowed his wife to leave after decades of struggle to save their marriage. He does not love her any less by letting her go. In fact, some might say that he has finally shown the greatest expression of devotion by putting her desires above his own. He wanted her to stay; she wanted to go. In similar fashion, final judgment is not the end of God's love; it is the final expression of love's commitment to our freedom, to the reality of our choices and to the integrity of our relationships. God never stops loving even those who finally reject heaven.

The language of love becomes nothing more than empty rhetoric if it is not regularly embodied in tangible actions. Even infinite love requires specific expression if it is not to become vapid. There comes a point when talk is cheap, especially if promises are never kept. In the same vein, there must also be some specific moment at which God's promise of eternal life is actualized for the faithful. That moment of decision is not the result of impatience but of faithfulness. God may potentially have limitless patience; the top half of the Creator's hourglass never runs out of sand. Yet, at the same time, God has also made a commitment that one day all the faithful will be brought into a new home constructed of eternal goodness. God grows tired of waiting, but this weariness is not the fruit of diminished endurance but of unfaltering devotion. Eventually, God must decide: "Now is the moment to keep my word."

Last night my teaching job required me to attend the annual honors convocation for our graduating seniors. I ignored the various memos reminding me that I was expected to attend because my youngest daughter was playing her flute and singing (not at the same time) in a school recital that evening. In deciding to keep a commitment to my daughter, I may have upset certain college administrators, but that's the way it goes. As Abraham Lincoln once said, "You can please all of the people some of the time, and some of the people all of the time, but you can never please all of the people all of the time." Not even God can please all of the people all of the time as long as personal relationships occur in time and space, involve promise and fulfilment requiring give and take. And since this is what God is committed to—real relationship, established in freedom, cultivated through offering and response—there will never be a moment in time when the entire human race will offer unrestricted, universal surrender. On this side of the eternal divide, there never has been and never will be any single moment of utopian bliss. Unfortunately, somebody, somewhere will always be holding out; someone will always be waiting to be punished. Even as I finish writing this illustration, I am struck by its inadequacy; yet, despite the weaknesses of the comparison, I think we can grasp the point: for God to wait endlessly for everyone to believe would be to renege on the promises of eternity.

The third objection sounds something like this: it appears irresponsible for God to give us a choice between two options when we are constitutionally incapable of comprehending the significance of the choice being made. How can we, mere mortals, be expected to understand the eternal ramifications of our earthly decisions? How can we be held accountable for implications we never imagined? If God were to treat us this way, it would be comparable to the modern proponents of chaos theory holding Amazonian butterflies accountable for the destruction created by hurricane Rita.[13] Similarly, no sensible person punishes a three year old playing with a loaded gun found hidden in daddy's bedside drawer; blame the irresponsible father for his foolishness. So to, is it unreasonable to blame people for the unforeseen, eternal repurcussions of personal choices; blame the God who foolishly entrusted decisions of eternal life and death to mere mortals.

This final objection might have some force to it if two things could be proven. First, eternal judgment might, indeed, be unfair if it were truly impossible for us to ever understand the lasting implications of our earthly decisions. In that case, such judgment would be very much like smashing butterflies for causing hurricanes, or slapping neglected toddlers for tumbling down the stairs. Second, judgment might also be unfair if God had never made a realistic, good faith attempt to explain the lasting consequences of our decisions. Without prior warning or explanation, it is hard to see how God could fairly hold us accountable for our mistakes.

But this is, in fact, exactly what God has tried to do. We cannot accuse God of unfairness because there have been repeated attempts at explanation. When I explain to my small child the importance of not playing near the hot stove, I cannot reasonably expect a 5 year old to comprehend the searing heat of the burner or the disfigurement that could result from spilling a pan of boiling water, but I can hope to communicate a clear sense of danger and warning. I can also expect my child to pay attention. Hopefully, parental instruction, combined with my attempts to maintain a safe kitchen, will prevent any accidents from happening, although there are no guarantees. If I placed my child's hand into a pot of boiling water in order to illustrate my warning, I would be guilty of child abuse not creative parenting. I might argue that I was acting in my child's best interests, but I doubt if many would be convinced. Protesting to the judge that my warnings alone could never adequately convey the dangers of boiling water would not be a defense. Scalding a child is never acceptable under any circumstances, despite the fact that it may be the only way for anyone to learn what it actually feels like to be burned. I know that I never took my mother's warnings as seriously as I did after accidentally burning a stovetop spiral into the palm of my hand.

What is God to do with us? Short of actually dipping us momentarily into an instant of eternal punishment, how can God offer an effective warning about the dangers of persistent disobedience? And what guarantee do we have that even this would be effective for everyone? I imagine that we all know of at least one strong-willed child who kept going back for more no matter how many times he was warned, punished or taken to the emergency room. Consequently, it strikes me as very unfair to say that God is unjust in allowing us to suffer the consequences of our actions simply because we may not be capable of fully grasping all their implications. Actually, God has gone to great lengths to warn us quite graphically. In the Christian tradition, that warning is most poignantly found in the cross at Calvary.

The crucifixion of Jesus Christ has always been the centerpiece of any Christian explanation of God's dealings with the world. At this precise moment in history the infinite love of God and the inescapable justice of God collided in the disfigured body of Jesus of Nazareth, our willing sacrifice. History has always been the arena in which God works out divine revelation. Some two thousand years ago a man who had done nothing but live a perfect life of continual obedience to his Creator hung from a Roman cross after a bogus trial where he had been convicted on false charges. After six hours of hanging in the Middle Eastern sun, Jesus cried out:

> My God, my God, why have you forsaken me? (Mark 15:34)

The one human being who had always done everything right, who had every reason to anticipate God's embrace, now saw only the backside of an alienated Creator's hasty exit. And he asks, "Why, God? Why?"

Imagine the perfect marriage, where a man and woman really do love each other unconditionally, sacrificially, expressing their devotion in a thousand and one acts of unpremeditated kindness every day. If you asked them at the end of the day to describe for you how they had shown their love, they probably could not remember the half of it, because their affection flowed so naturally, so spontaneously, that the left hand seldom knew what the right hand was doing. It was as if they could read each other's minds and anticipate the other's next move before they knew it themselves. They were one—one heart, one mind, one flesh.

Such a relationship may be an idealistic dream that few, if any, of us ever attain in this world, but I have known a few who certainly thought they had come close. At least, they imagined that their relationship was as close to perfection as they could ever expect in this lifetime; marriage surpassed all their dreams. I have also held a few of their hands the morning after, when they woke up to discover a scribbled note on the kitchen counter saying that the relationship was over, that the partner was tired of living a sham. They were flattened by a train they never saw coming. If you had stood the abandoned person against a brick wall and hired Babe Ruth to swing his bat at their heart with all of his might, you could not have seen greater pain than the grief I have observed in the vacant stares of these abandoned men and women. Of course, a good therapist could point out the warning signs, evident but overlooked; hindsight is always 20/20. But subsequent explanations never lessen the shock of an unforeseen blow to the head.

Let's try to suspend our scepticism for just a moment and entertain the possibility that Jesus of Nazareth was a man who enjoyed precisely this type of ideal relationship with God, a life of unbroken, moment-by-moment communion. The intimacy was not imaginary or one-sided. He was not misguided. There were no warning signs to miss, only a perfect relationship of mutual love and response such as God had always wanted with each of us. And then, suddenly, without warning, out of the blue, the peace, the meaning and fulfilment, the sublime sense of tranquility born of knowing down in the very marrow of your bones that you are unconditionally loved and accepted—all of that was ripped out of him and for the first time in his life, at the moment of his deepest need, Jesus found himself empty and alone. The question, "My God, my God, why have you abandoned me?" expresses the puzzlement of one who suddenly finds himself on the opposite side of the divide. Though there is no explicit Biblical warrant for the line in the Apostle's Creed saying that Jesus "descended into hell," it rightly expresses the profound horror of one who finds himself permanently separated from God.[14] In the death-cry of this carpenter from Galilee, we see the internal collision of heavenly dreams and earthly reality that constitutes eternal torment.

At that moment, the punishment of all human rebellion throughout history was heaped upon the shoulders of this one man, the one the Christian church calls the God-man. Divine justice will not be denied. The retribution demanded by our own righteous indignation—the punishment of evil, the recompense for atrocity, the full measure of judgment for crimes against humanity—was poured out upon the head of the perfect Son of God. Holy justice was executed at the cross so that divine mercy may be shown to everyone who receives its benefits by faith. This is the Christian gospel that finally answers the question of how love, justice and relationship may all eventually intersect in eternity. Jesus experienced God's weariness historically so that you and I may benefit from God's patience eternally; unless, of course, we refuse the offer. In which case, each of us will one day confront God's weariness alone. According to the New Testament, the death of Jesus Christ provides both God's warning about the consequences of rebellion as well as the solution to our dilemna of being imperfect people in search of a perfect God

Abraham Heschel has written that God's weariness is exhibited when "divine anger becomes active in history."[15] From a Christian perspective, the cross becomes the paradoxical, historical moment when God became weary with God. God's anger from heaven was directed against God in the world. And because Jesus is the Son of God who suffered God's weariness, he is now able to extend an invitation: "Come to me, all you who are weary and worn down, and I will give you rest" (Matthew 11:2).

6

SITUATIONS REAL AND IMAGINED

Are We Projecting Our Emotions onto God?

*We can only come to view ourselves through the
eyes of those who view us.*
—Michael Lewis, *Shame: The Exposed Self*

I feel so ashamed of my thoughts. I'm sure God isn't too impressed with me. I tried to commit suicide before and I promised him never again, and yet somehow here I am again, not wanting to do it but wanting to be with him and away from my life down here. I feel so tired . . . I want so badly to be with Jesus and I can't find him down here. I try to talk to him about how I feel . . . but sometimes I feel as if he has left me completely. When I need him the most, when I can't communicate that to him, I feel alone . . . I'm torn between being angry with God and begging for his mercy. I don't know how or what to pray. I know that I have to just keep reaching for him and not give up.

It was the first time anyone had shown me their scars or written me a letter as gut-wrenching as the excerpt above. There were two jagged, red slashes across the wrists, still looking very fresh, far from healed. As the young woman rolled her sleeves back down, she repeated through her tears, "I'm so ashamed. God must hate me."

"No. Never," I said. "God will never hate you. God loves you deeply—always has, always will."

"How can I ever believe that?"

The woman sitting across the table from me went on to tell about previous attempts to end it all. Suicidal depression had become a well-known companion throughout much of her young life. I eventually discovered that someone—I suspect a religious authority figure from the past—had once told her that her inability to experience God's love was a punishment. Her depression was divine retribution, heaven's scourge against the ungrateful. God had abandoned her because she had committed the unforgiveable sin; she had tried to kill herself. Now she was unable to find God because God had turned away, leaving her to bear the weight of her shame alone. That crushing weight had caused her to try again just a few weeks earlier. Fortunately, she had second thoughts, found help and was taken to the emergency room before it was too late.

How my friend felt about herself and what she believed about God's feelings towards her were inextricably intertwined with each other. In this regard, she was hardly unique. Since I knew that we shared many of the same basic, religious convictions, I urged her to believe that whoever had told her such things in the past had lied. God did not hate her, not even for attempting suicide. Neither was her depression a punishment for anything she had ever done. Not only had God not abandoned her, but she was so deeply loved that God wept with her through her depression. God grieved over her grief and desired her healing more than she could imagine.

Occasionally we are given the privilege of witnessing one of those magical moments when something momentous happens in another person's life. For whatever reason, a light seemed to go on for my friend. A look of timidity blended with hopefulness flashed over her tear-stained face.

"Really?" she asked.

"Really," I said.

This was the first time she had ever been told that her pain was not God's angry indictment. Her thoughts about herself were not an automatic reflection of God's feelings towards her.

"You mean God can really love me *like this*?"

I told her what I have been pleased to tell many others before and since, "Yes. Yes. Yes. God loves you exactly the way you are."

Fortunately, with the ongoing help of counseling and medication, my friend is now almost unrecognizable when compared to my memory of the woman who showed me her scars. Unfortunately, the confusion of issues involved in her struggle with God are all too common. Normally, we interpret another's emotional disposition by reading the complex signals sent to us by facial expression, body movement, tone of voice and vocabulary. However, how do we learn to discern the emotional state of someone we have never physically seen or heard? How are we to intuit God's emotional posture towards us at any particular moment? Not many can claim to have actually seen visions or heard voices from heaven. Although I realize that occasionally someone will claim exactly that, right now I am thinking about the majority of average people to whom God has always remained invisible and inaudible. Professor Michael Lewis has written that "coping with the emotional life of each individual is the major task of relationships."[1] If this is true, and I think it is, then how are we ever to develop a deeper relationship with an invisible God? It is the premise of this book that God is an emotional Being available for personal interaction with each of us. Yet, the supreme Otherness that attracts us to God also appears to create an unbridgeable chasm that makes genuine intimacy impossible. How can I learn to "cope" with something I can never perceive? And how do I learn to perceive the emotional life of a deity devoid of any audible or visual emotional cues?

The prospects of true relationship with such a God would seem to be hopeless were it not for the fact that our innate spiritual hunger refuses to be satisfied with placeboes. Consequently, we instinctively look to our other personal relationships in a search for analogies to our connection with God, hoping that our interaction with someone we understand (spouse or roommate) will offer guidance for relating to someone we do not understand (God). A lifetime of experience in these types of relationships tells us that people engage in emotional give and take. There is a cause-and-effect relationship between my emotional life and the other person's behavior.[2] I generally feel loved in response to being loved. I typically feel rejected in response to being rejected. Our natural assumption, based upon these cummulative experiences, is to assume that our life situation is somehow the result of God's disposition towards us. If I feel rejected by God, it must be because I have been rejected; therefore, I can know that God is disinterested in me. If I feel unloved by God, it must be because God does not love me; therefore, the only divine emotions I can hope to experience are God's anger or indifference. While my friend had the misfortune of actually being told by someone she trusted that her depression was the result of God's punishment, this assessment also agreed with her natural inclination. If she felt that she was worthless, it must have been because God had actually reached the same verdict and rejected her already.

Of course, miscommunication is all too common in any relationship, even with our closest friends. When I misunderstand my wife's intentions or respond to her overtures inappropriately, she is readily available to correct my blunder (which she does freely). But who corrects my misunderstandings of God?

THINKING ABOUT WHAT OTHERS THINK ABOUT YOU

At the turn of the century a psychologist by the name of Charles Cooley coined the term "the looking-glass self."[3] The looking-glass self is composed of three elements: my imagination of how I appear to another person; my imagination of how the other person judges my appearance; and the resulting feeling I develop about myself. Most of us view the world as such a looking-glass self. In this looking-glass world, my self-image is not a matter of who I think I am; nor is it a matter of who you think I am; it is a matter of who I think you think I am. You will notice that there are a tremendous number of assumptions being made in this looking-glass world, assumptions about impressions, responses, attitudes and judgments, all resulting in the formation of a person's self-image—the image we think we see looking back at us in the mirror.

When I began my doctoral program in Great Britain, before I learned that British academics were no different than anyone else, I labored under a distinct inferiority complex. Surely, I thought, it was only a matter of time before someone discovered that I was an American fraud. How could anyone from "the colonies" hope to compete against graduates of Oxford, Cambridge and Edinburgh? I imagined that I appeared to be an obvious, intellectual light-weight to my British classmates. I also imagined that they judged me as falling far short of the normal standards for doctoral students. Consequently, I was very self-conscious, to say the least, especially during my first academic year. I often thought of Groucho Marx's famous remark about reconsidering his membership in any club that would allow him in as a member. Whenever I ventured to make a hesitant comment in our post-graduate seminars, I immediately interpreted any subsequent pause in the conversation as a verdict on my contribution; obviously, whatever I had said was so ridiculous that it did not merit a response. As a result, I felt that my initial fears were regularly confirmed. If someone had told me that the pause was only natural as people collected their thoughts, or that they were momentarily considering my insight, I would have rejected this analysis out of hand. I knew better. My imaginary fears confirmed by interpretation, and my interpretation reconfirmed my fears.

When one's framework for interpreting his or her place in the world is this coherent, always producing the answer you had expected, it seldom occurs to you that the whole thing just might be terribly irrational to begin with, and that its complete predictability is the very piece of evidence that ought to make you most suspicious. Eventually, after receiving enough positive feedback on my work and seeing that it was at least as good as anyone else's, I began to reevaluate my imaginary fears. Apparently, I was not inherently inferior to all British doctoral students as I initially suspected. However, for people with looking-glass problems such as mine, these moments of sanity are brief; it only took a few seconds for me to suspect that had I gone to Germany, instead of Scotland, I certainly would have been inferior to all German doctoral candidates! Aha!

Notice the similarity between the thinking process of the looking-glass self and the way that my friend in the introduction had imagined her relationship with God. First, she imagined how she must have appeared to God (unlovable). Second, she then imagined God's judgment upon such an unlovable person (rejection). Finally, she adopted the appropriate feelings about and responses towards this unlovable person rejected by God (deeper depression). Ironically, when Charles Cooley made these insightful observations about the development of self-image, he was not analyzing religion or religious experience; he was describing the psychological mechanism that produces shame. I find this to be a fascinating coincidence. The common, reflexive response for what a person believes God feels towards her is strikingly reminiscent of the process whereby she will also experience shame. Experiencing God and feeling shame seem to transpire along parallel tracks in the human psyche—an observation that raises an important question. How do I ever know which process is operating? When I feel worthless or rejected by God, am I experiencing God's evaluation of me or my evaluation of myself? When I come to feel that God is angry with me and intent upon punishing me, is it really God's verdict or is it my own belief that I deserve to be rejected because of some unrecognized, hidden sense of shame? How do I tell the difference between God's feelings towards me and my own feelings about myself?

SPIRITUALITY AND THE HUMAN SPIRIT

No contraptions are more complex that a human being. We may have mapped the human genome, but we are a long way from knowing how to build a person from scratch, and no part of our humanity is more complex than the mind. In fact, the more we learn about human consciousness, the more mysterious the mind becomes. One philosopher, Colin McGinn, has gone so far as to conclude that it is intrinsically impossible for the human mind to ever understand itself.[4] It is an impossible task. As thinking, feeling human beings, you and I are an enigma locked in a mystery wrapped in a riddle. Fascinating, recent discoveries continue to stir the mix further when it comes to parsing out the spiritual and emotional ingredients of the thinking person. For example, current research in neuroscience (the study of the brain) has overturned the ancient dichotomy between reason and emotion, thinking and feeling, demonstrating that the ability to think clearly is dependant upon healthy, functional emotional responses to life's circumstances. Far from being separate, distinct functions of the brain, we now know that if the part of my brain that instructs me in how to respond emotionally to a situation is not functioning properly, I will not be able to analyze it properly, either. Dr. Antonio Damasio has even intimated that human emotion may need to be given center-stage in the quest for unpacking human rationality. His best-selling book, *Descarte's Error: Emotion, Reason, and the Human Brain*, suggests that when the French father of modern philosophy Rene Descarte (A.D. 1596-1650) declared, "I think, therefore, I am!" he was actually confusing thinking with feeling.[5] It is not our reason but our capacity to experience and express emotion that anchors us in the real world. Our thinking ability is yoked with our ability to feel emotion, and the emotions we experience are tied to the processes by which we think. It is only a short step from Dr. Damasio's new, neurobiological dictum, "I feel, therefore, I am" to our own psychological hall of mirrors, "How I feel is how I think I am."

Similarly, there is an increasingly close connection being forged between neurobiology, psychology and spiritual experience. For example, there is almost certainly a genetic component to an individual's susceptibility to both shame and depression.[6] Similarly, a good deal of research indicates that people prone to depression are also more likely to wrestle with debilitating shame.[7] Depression and shame like to cohabit. Apparently, some of us are more melancholy and shame-prone than others, not only because of how our parents may have raised us but also because of the genetic material they had to work with. But if there is a genetic component to depression and shame, could there also be a genetic component to religious sensibility? In other words, might some people be more sensitive to experiencing the presence of God because of their biological makeup? Could the value of prayer have as much to do with brain chemistry as it does the power of faith?

Believe it or not, many researchers today insist that it does. For instance, a Canadian psychologist named Dr. Michael Pensinger attached himself to a machine called a transcranial magnetic stimulator and claimed to experience God for the first time in his life.[8] The TMS is a helmet-like device that, when attached to the scalp, can target a high-powered, fluctuating magnetic field onto discreet portions of the brain, thereby activating it and giving some indication of its function. For example, if you stimulated parts of the motor cortex, certain muscles would contract causing your arm to twitch or your leg to flex. Dr. Pensinger targeted his temporal lobes which is also the part of the brain central to processing emotional experience. Guess what happened. Dr. Pensinger published the results of his experiment and said that he had finally experienced God. Although he did not describe whether he heard a voice or saw a vision, he insisted that he profoundly felt the presence of the divine.

Medical researchers have known for years that people who have epileptic seizures, especially those that originate in the left side of the temporal lobe, regularly describe intense, spiritual experiences sometimes resulting in personality changes that may last long after the seizures have ended.[9] Such people may claim to see God or to have received insight into the mysteries of the universe. Psychiatrists have also long observed the similarities between certain types of psychosis and religious forms of mystical experience.[10] Dr. Vilayanur Ramachandran, one of the leading neurobiological researchers in the world today, arrives at, what are for me, two particularly interesting conclusions: first, there are clearly "circuits" in the human brain that are intricately involved in religious experience; and, second, it is "ironic" that the "sense of enlightenment...that Truth is revealed... should derive from (brain structures) concerned with emotions rather than from the thinking, rational parts of the brain that take so much pride in their ability to discern truth and falsehood."[11] How interesting. Apparently, our religious circuitry is intertwined with our emotional processing units which in turn are fundamental to our reasoning ability. Maybe it is more than coincidental that the way in which we typically intuit our emotional standing with God is mirrored in something like the shaming process, and that the debilitating emotion of shame is linked to the irrationality of the looking-glass self. The way I think, the way I feel, and the way I think God feels about me are all woven tightly together inside my psyche.

Naturally, some people will claim that all this research simply proves what they have known all along: that there is no God. According to these critics, what I call the experience of God is nothing more than overstimulated neurons in my temporal lobe firing more erradically than normal amidst an oversupply of the neurochemicals seratonine or dopamine. It is all in my head, literally. However, it is important to note that not all of the scientists themselves agree with this conclusion. Observing a phenomenon is a far cry from explaining it or knowing why it happens. Dr. Ramachandran, for instance, offers this analogy. Most animals are color-blind, lacking the visual receptors and neural components necessary for color vision. Only a relatively small percentage have the neurobiological mechanisms necessary to see the world in living color. Does this mean that color is not real? Must the colors of the rainbow be an illusion, an imaginary phenomenon created only in the animal's mind by its distinctive brain circuitry? Obviously not. Perhaps the frontal lobes are sometimes excited by the presence of a real God, just as the color receptors in our brain are stimulated by the real light waves allowing us to perceive color? Maybe, maybe not. In any case, the atheist's conclusion does not automatically follow from the scientist's observations.

A PERSONAL JOURNEY

For many years my own efforts to understand God's feelings towards me were tangled by the trip-wire of depression. Beginning in late adolescence, my life began to periodically slide through cycles of psychic bleakness. I had always been a loner growing up—partly because I was an Army-brat who moved more than an ant on a griddle—and I suppose those who knew me might have described me as moody. But somewhere around the time I graduated from high school and began college, these cycles evolved from adolescent self-pity into gray tunnels of despair. I could seldom anticipate the tunnel's approach; I simply woke up one morning to find myself lying in the dark. I may not have been able to see the tunnel's end, but I quickly learned that if I could stick it out long enough, the tunnel would eventually open up; I would break out into the fresh light of a new day, and the pleasures of life would return. In these dark periods, day to day existence became a disciplined process of forging ahead at all costs. Fortunately, whatever other qualities I may lack (I know the list is long), self-discipline is not one of them. While mechanically placing one foot in front of the other is not the most romantic or fulfilling way to live, at least it kept me going after every other motivation had evaporated.

My young wife learned to recognize the cycles and would feel me out by asking if I was having "one of my bouts." She could sense the gloom before I would. The fog descended so slowly, like the creep of an evening's twilight, that her question would often be my first hint that I had unknowingly wandered back into another of those caverns. Again, fortunately for me, she has always been exceedingly patient in living with a man who regularly came and went so unpredictably.

I am also thankful that we had children when we did. It is awfully easy to think about death when life feels so dead already. As I began to hit middle-age, the dark periods became darker and longer, the slices of blue sky grew slimmer and duller. I found myself thinking often about the guilt that suicide left behind for the surviving family members and how my children needed me even though I often felt like checking out. I figured that my wife could get along just fine without me; she is resilient. It was the inevitable damage to my children that kept me fighting against the periodic allure of putting an end to it all. Somewhere around my mid-thirties I hit a brick wall. This time the tunnel did not open up anymore, ever.

I was a Christian all throughout these years of struggle—a minister and community leader through much of it— but believing that I had a relationship with God was seldom of any help. In fact, it often seemed counter-productive. Like my depressed friend in the introduction, I too believed that I knew where I was going; the afterlife was no mystery for me. Thus death could be strangely appealling. In heaven I would finally be free of the darkness.

Furthermore, it was my life with God that caused me to feel most overloaded with the experience of failure and accusation; eventually, nagging, anonymous guilt became a never-ending state of mind. Knowing God was like falling through the rabbit hole with Alice in Wonderland. I was perpetually chasing after something that was always just slipping around the next bend. For years, from the moment my eyelids opened in the morning until they closed again at night, I would be haunted with a gnawing suspicion that somehow I had disappointed God. I could never explain how or why; I just felt it. Each day unfolded beneath the thick cover of anonymous accusation, never tied to anything specific, but always waiting there to remind me of my failure as a human being. I once told a friend that my life felt like a huge jigsaw puzzle where all the pieces looked exactly alike. Somehow or another my part of the puzzle was missing a few pieces; an exasperated God was waiting for me to find them and put them all in place. However, try as I might, I could never find those missing pieces of the puzzle. God knew where they were, and He was waiting, but I could never find the right answers. My life felt like one, long, endless search with no end in sight.

It was my daughter's tears that finally sent me to a therapist. Several friends had observed my decline and cared enough to broach the subject with me. (If only we all had such good people in our lives). A few even suggested that I was suffering from depression, an idea that I had always staunchly resisted. "This is not depression," I insisted. "It is just life; I happen to take things more seriously than most people"—at least, that is how I tried to convince myself everything was OK. Then one Saturday afternoon, as I was describing to my wife how hopeless it all seemed, I noticed my ten year old daughter eavesdropping from the dining room. Her wide eyes told me she had heard it all. As I walked over to put my arms around her, she burst into tears. It suddenly occurred to me that although I had managed to spare by children the trauma of dealing with a father's suicide, I was unwittingly putting them through a more protracted turmoil by raising them as a depressed person who would not get help.

When Monday arrived I made an appointment to see my doctor.

I will never forget driving home from that appointment. I cried like a baby trying to watch the road through a veil of tears. My doctor diagnosed me as suffering from clinical depression. He wrote a prescription for an antidepressant and made a referral to a psychotherapist. I cried, in part, because I was ashamed. I was ashamed of not being able to make myself feel better. I was ashamed because this sort of thing was not supposed to happen to people who loved God. Admitting to depression was just one more failure in my life, and to be told that I needed medication, well that was admitting to mental illness. I was especially ashamed of that obvious, psychological flaw. What had I done to deserve this? Yet, there was another part of me that cried for joy. Finally, someone had put a name to what I had been trying to deal with for so many years, and if it could be identified, then maybe it could be solved. I now experienced a tentative sense of hopefulness and anticipation that would incrementally usher me into virgin territory of emotional well-being.

I will spare you all the details. Suffice it to say that after a number of years of periodic counselling, both with my wife and without her, individually and in groups, my life has taken on an entirely different cast. In particular, my experiences helped me to gleen a few insights into the process of distinguishing between God's disposition towards me and the confused misapprehensions of my own looking-glass self. Exploring these distinctions requires that we first look into the problem of guilt and shame.

GOD, GUILT AND SHAME

I was speaking about the concept of divine fatherhood at a retreat for Canadian college students. After one of the evening sessions, I noticed a young lady with short blond hair lingering hesitantly near the back of the auditorium. I had a suspicion that she wanted to talk but was waiting for the crowd to clear out so our conversation would not be overheard. My suspicions were correct. As the crowd trickled away, I stayed behind. Eventually, she slowly moved forward; I went to meet her halfway. After introducing herself, she told me that she had recently begun to learn about Christianity and was intrigued by what she was discovering about the immense love God had shown to her in Jesus Christ. However, she then went on to say that, even though she was attracted to the idea of Jesus as her savior and friend, the thought of God as her father sent shivers down her spine.

I anticipated the next part of her story. As you might have guessed, she had been sexually abused by her father. Now, she literally became physically ill when she associated an all powerful God with the idea of fatherhood, for it was her father who had destroyed her childhood by turning intimacy into incest. Would God do something similar? The anguish in her face told me that she was not exaggerating. I could also see that inside she harbored the shame and guilt typical of the abused, having convinced herself as a child that somehow the pain daddy inflicted was her fault. What could she do?

For the time being, I told her that it was perfectly appropriate to forget about God-as-father and to focus her attention upon the loving Jesus who had already begun to change her life. But before our long conversation was over, I also urged her to find the counselling help she needed so that one day she might learn to disentangle the memories of her earthly father from the waiting reality of the heavenly father who would never do anything but love her. At that moment, she could not believe that this would ever be possible, but I still have hope.

My suicidal friend, this young Canadian woman, and my own experience with depression all have a lot in common. Upbringing, personality, genetics, and learning to distinguish the true from the false are all essential ingredients for each of us in becoming healthy. Particularly important is an understanding of how the travelling companions called guilt and shame operate in a person's life. In discussing these two emotions, we wade neck deep into swift waters with many conflicting cross-currents. For example, there is a significant debate over exactly how to define the two emotions, as well as how to explain their relationship to each other.[12] Fortunately, for our purposes, I believe we can uncover the information we need without getting bogged down in all the fine print.

Most psychologists agree that shame concerns one's sense of self, whereas guilt has to do with behavior.[13] A sense of shame raises questions about self-worth and personhood; it involves several key components: the status of personal relationships; the social customs binding those relationships together; and the acceptable boundaries of self-exposure (whether physical, intellectual or emotional) within those relationships. Shame arises from the sense of being diminished in front of others, of being shown to be personally inadequate. Guilt, on the other hand, is concerned with breaking ethical boundaries and the resulting sense of personal responsibility to right the wrong. Consequently, it may result in such acts as confession and restitution. "Guilt is the inner experience of breaking the moral code. Shame is the inner experience of being looked down upon by the social group."[14] Having said this, however, we must quickly point out that, as with most things in life, shame and guilt do not remain isolated in discreet boxes.[15]

First of all, shame and guilt easily overlap such that I can feel both ashamed and guilty about the same things. How many times have you impetuously done something out of character only to think to yourself accusingly, "What kind of person am I to do such a thing?" We interpret our behavior as an expression of who we are, and our sense of self is tied up with how we behave making it impossible to neatly segregate the one from the other. Personality and choices are always grafted together.

Second, just because shame finds its roots in the social dynamics of personal relationship does not mean that I will only experience shame in the face of another person's overt disapproval. Remember the power of the looking-glass self. I do not have to know for certain that you disapprove of me in order to feel ashamed in front of you; all I have to do is imagine that I appear to you in a shameful light, and then imagine further that you have disapproved, and my resulting shame will be every bit as real as if I had been publicly flogged in the village square. Not only do I internalize the social expectations of the world around me—this is the way I form my conscience—but my looking-glass self also internalizes a hundred and one different imaginary voices, the voices of family, friends, co-workers, supervisors, neighbors, you name it, all telling me what I think that person must be thinking about me. I attribute to others the internalized feelings of self-scorn that I have come to believe about myself. I can be ashamed and guilty both publicly and privately, in truth as well as in my imagination.

My Canadian friend had internalized the disparaging voice of her father and further confused it with the voice of God. This is another common mistake. In the early stages of childhood, the parent basically is god to a growing child. An infant is totally dependent upon the parents to provide for all her basic needs. Life and death, literally, hang upon a parent's care. Not surprisingly, when a spiritual quest later in life leads us to consider our dependence upon God, we may unwittingly transfer the childhood expectations created by our own parents onto our new, adult expectations of the divine. If we are not attentive to this unconscious transition, we can easily create a distorted image of our Creator without ever realizing what we have done. We will simply find ourselves inexplicably condemned by the imaginary voices of relatives and others, as well as the imaginary voice of an unreal God, thus misconstruing our own inner demons as the voice of our Creator.

Needless to say, civilized society and personal well-being depend upon the healthy operation of legitimate shame and appropriate guilt. There are times when it is necessary for us to be caught in the grip of both emotions. Our humanity depends upon it.[16] There are moments when I am genuinely guilty, and I ought to be ashamed of myself. The challenge is learning to distinguish the healthy from the unhealthy, the true from the false, the real from the imaginary. This process of discrimination is at the heart of cultivating personal well-being and a genuine knowledge of the one, true God.

Cutting through this mess of psychological entanglements lay at the heart of my own treatment for depression—that and Prozac. Once my doctor heard me describe my history with depression, he immediately suspected that it had both physical and psychological dimensions. He was right. Hardly a day goes by when I do not thank God for the marvels of modern medicine. Earlier we discovered that shame-prone personalities may have a biological basis and that the variety of our emotional and spiritual experiences are (at least) partially controlled by our brain chemistry, whether in the temporal lobes or elsewhere. I have no doubt that this is true in my case. Anti-depressant medication has been essential to the progress of my own emotional and spiritual well-being. Medication by itself did not silence the haunting accusations of shame, guilt and failure, but it did switch on a new light inside the tunnel so that, for the first time, I could begin to confront my internal accusers, tear the masks from the imposters and learn to attend to the authentic voices.

Since this is not a book about psychotherapy, I will not go into the details of what it takes to actually sort through the complicated issues of false shame and inappropriate guilt.[17] The best step you can take is to find a good therapist, someone who shares your basic world-view, someone with whom you can have a trusting rapport, and begin the hard spade-work of actually exploring your inner life. Hopefully, for our purposes, a basic awareness of the complex influences arising from biology, brain chemistry, family background, environment, upbringing, self-esteem and current life situation will be sufficient to help you understand how easily—almost unavoidably—we can confuse the voice of God with the murmurings of our private ghosts.

KNOWING AND BEING KNOWN

In discussing guilt and shame, we come to the first of the emotions that are not reciprocated by God. Because we were made in God's image, every other human emotion discussed thus far has been analogous to an emotion within the Creator. We both experience comparable forms of anger, jealousy and disappointment, for example. We are free to enquire into these similarities as long as we remember Tertullian's maxim about viewing God as the perfect model and ourselves as the imperfect reflection; the correspondence is not exact. Biblical religion also makes it clear that this reciprocity vanishes once we come upon the stumbling blocks of guilt and shame.[18] God never experiences either, although there are moments when God has legitimate reason to be *a*shamed of us. We have not thoroughly addressed the spiritual dimension of our guilt/shame dilemma until we explore this final dimension of shame.

Biblical religion has never drawn the sharp distinction between personhood (as the focus of shame) and behavior (as the focus of guilt) made by modern psychology. Consequently, the Bible regularly talks about people being both shamed and guilty because of their actions. The Old and New Testaments regularly ask the question, "What kind of person would do such a thing?" And, indeed, the consistent answer is, "A guilty person who ought to feel ashamed of himself." When I lie to my boss and take credit for another employee's work, I make myself a liar; a healthy conscience also ought to make me feel guilty (for, as we have already seen, there can be a big difference between *being* guilty and *feeling* guilty), and I probably ought to feel ashamed as well. The Bible definitely tells me that I should be ashamed. However, having said this, I am not about to take back everything I just discussed regarding the destructive power of false guilt and shame. The challenge is to achieve the proper alignment between being and feeling, alignment within myself about myself, as well as alignment within myself about my relationship to God. So, after all this time, we return once again to our initial question about accurately discerning another person's attitude towards us. I said before that typically we read things like facial expression, body movement, tone of voice and vocabulary in order to intuit the other person's emotional disposition. When your friend wrinkles her nose, you have discovered over time that this means she is frustrated with you. Even though God does not leave that kind of relational residue from body language or vocal intonation, the Creator has left us with a great deal of specific vocabulary in the Bible. As we have already seen, the Old and New Testaments purport to record the long history of God's self-description comprised of a very specific selection of words and phrases. Literally, tens of thousands of surviving manuscripts allow us to recreate the original, ancient texts with amazing accuracy. Consequently, we can safely say that those who want to know how God feels about them have not been left in the dark. The question for the Judaeo-Christian tradition, then, becomes: "How does the Bible describe God's disposition towards me as a person? How does God view my selfhood?" Counselling can help tremendously in disentangling the complications that work to obscure my understanding of God, but in the final analysis only God's own words are able to speak the truth about how God feels towards me. So, what has God said?

The Bible tells us that after learning everything there is to know about us, including all of our deepest, darkest secrets, God loves us unconditionally without hesitation. This eternal love is directed at our person irrespective of our actions; God certainly does not approve of everything we do, but love of our person is permanent and absolute. Whatever voices from the past have become confused with God's, we can always be certain that any voice, real or imagined, telling us that God is disinterested is the deceit of our own or someone else's looking-glass self. So the apostle Paul declares:

> I am positive that nothing can separate us from God's love—not life or death, not angels or spirits, not the present or the future, not powers above or powers below. Nothing in all creation can separate us from God's love for us in Christ Jesus. (Romans 8:38-39)

If my experience is typical, then the most profound desire motivating each of us through life's relational landscape is the yearning to be fully, completely known and accepted. Discovering this type of relationship is difficult. It is one of the reasons we hide our dirty laundry and keep our secrets to ourselves. If such memories engender shame and guilt within me, then what can I reasonably expect from everybody else? Part of the reason we are seldom completely known, then, is that we rarely feel secure enough to risk airing all of our dark secrets with others. We do not allow ourselves to be known. We are regularly intimidated by the bogeyman of shame. Here is the paradox: the more another person means to you, the more you want to share yourself openly and to be fully known, but since there is also so much more at stake if the loved one is repelled by your secrets, the more hesitant you are to open those locked closets. Unresolved shame becomes toxic to true intimacy.

Take Marcia, for example. She has fallen in love with Roger, who is a very conservative guy. Marcia had been a wild teenager who got herself into more than her fair share of adolescent scrapes before eventually settling down to become the healthy, mature woman she is today. But she has a secret: she had an abortion her senior year of high school. Something inside of her cannot bear the thought of becoming any more intimate with Roger without first sharing this ancient part of her life. But she is also terrified that once he learns about her past, he will never want to see her again. She is caught between the proverbial rock and a hard place. Of course, a friend might tell her that if Roger reacts this way, then the relationship was not meant to be which is probably good advice. But that does not calm the nausea rumbling in the pit of Marcia's stomach.

Buried deep inside each of us is the burning desire to be fully known. True love is not simply a matter of another person revealing the entirety of themselves to you—such that you are given access to intimate recesses few, if any, have ever seen before; love is also a matter of someone else exploring your hidden corners, both delightful and repugnant, and becoming more devoted and enthralled rather than less. Such love means that you are free to abandon the familiar fear of rejection, and even to shed your lingering shame once and for all, because someone knows all that there is to know and loves you anyway just the way you are.

UNCOVERING THE GOD WHO DWELLS WITHIN

Knowing the truth about yourself and hearing the true voice of God coincide at the same intersection of the soul. God's uniqueness, the same uniqueness that can make relating to the divine so difficult and confusing, also allows us to explore alternatives not available in any other personal relationship. For example, until now I have been talking about relating to God exclusively in terms of a Me–You relationship (what the Jewish philosopher Martin Buber called the *I–Thou* relationship), as if the Creator were an identifiable Being located at a specific point on the map in front of me. However, such spatial language is always symbolic when used to describe the Creator. Where and how is God located? As Spirit, God is everywhere and nowhere, simultaneously. God is in front of me, behind me, but also *within me* in the same instant; even as the Spirit is within me, I also dwell within the Spirit as the apostle Paul reminded the ancient, Athenian philosophers: "In God we live and move and have our being!" (Acts 17:28).

The complications inherent in locating God are part and parcel of our continuing struggle to discern God's true feelings towards us. My so-called awareness of the divine is composed entirely of personal impressions, and impressions only happen inside of me, not outside. An impression outside of me is someone else's impression, not mine. So, somehow, I am forced to search my own, internal, personal impressions in order to discover God's attitudes towards me!? How can that be? It sounds a bit like studying for an exam by making up my own course outline. Therein lies the rub, a rub that hopefully has not been made raw by my various attempts to approach the problem from different angles. Fortunately, sometimes along with the rub there may come a shine. In this case, the shine produced by our struggle to hear God's voice also allows us to discover the reflection of God's presence within.

Many Christian writers throughout the history of the church have grasped the irony of this situation. Exploring that irony's potential for successfully advancing our quest after God is a distinctive feature of the long tradition of Christian mysticism. They understand better than most that reaching upward for God requires turning inward. The similarities between the mystic's attempt to turn inward in her quest for the divine, and our need to look inward for the discovery of God's verdict on our lives, suggests that the mystics may provide valuable insights for spiritual pilgrims such as ourselves. Although there are many teachers to whom we could turn, no one has done a better job of offering useful guidelines for those who search inside themselves than the 16th century Carmelite nun, Teresa of Ávila (A.D. 1515—1582).

THE FIRST MOTHER TERESA

The *Interior Castle* is Teresa's classic work on internal, spiritual exploration. This masterful guide through the personal corridors of mystical prayer is one of the most widely published Spanish works ever written, second only perhaps to the immortal *Don Quixote* by Cervantes.[19] Teresa, canonized as a saint by the Roman Catholic church only forty years after her death, had intimate experience in answering the questions we are wrestling with in this chapter. In fact, one modern authority has written that "Teresa's brilliant self-criticisms are our best source of information" on learning to distinguish the genuine voice of God from the many psychological counterfeits waiting to deceive the seeker.[20]

Teresa's childhood and family background did not make her an obvious candidate for eventual sainthood. Born of questionable legitimacy to a family scrambling to make a name for itself among the Spanish nobility, Teresa's brothers set off as soldiers of fortune during the Spanish conquests of the New World where at least one had his dreams extinguished by uncooperative South American natives. This passion for adventure was not limited to the males of the family. Teresa was also a hopeless romantic. At the age of five or six she set off on foot to join the war against the invading Moors, the "infidels," hoping that she might be given the privilege of dying a martyr's death. Fortunately, she was found by a frantic uncle before getting too far down the road and promptly returned to her worried father. Since she could not go to war, she turned her imagination to the legendary world of knights and damsels in distress becoming an avid reader of the medieval equivalents of our Harlequin romance novels, a passion inherited from her young mother. Eventually, a series of indiscreet late-night rendezvous with a young admirerer sent rumours circulating throughout the village. Fearing for his daughter's reputation, Teresa's father sent her to live in a nearby convent. From such inauspicious beginnings, legendary seeds are sometimes sown.

Though initially brought by force, Teresa would eventually make the religious life her consuming passion. Her visionary experiences and other "raptures," as she called them, only began after many years of prayerful devotion. Reading her writings makes it clear that such experiences were actually quite sporadic, far from daily events; however, her descriptions and analyses of these mystical experiences—experiences in which she might fall into a trance, receive a vision of Christ, be given a message by God—are so clinically dispassionate that the reader is compelled to believe her claims of the miraculous even as she pleaded with God to take the experiences away. She had good reason to fear. Her writings brought her to the attention of the Spanish Inquisition, and even though she was never officially branded a heretic, many viewed her with suspicion until long after her death.

The *Interior Castle* describes the fragile process of discovering the Spirit of God within oneself by becoming sensitively attuned to

God's transforming work. The castle is the soul with God seated in the center upon a throne. Since God resides within the same heart as her emotions, Teresa's crucial question is: How can she know if her spiritual experiences are genuine or misguided? Are the internal voices from God or her own imagination? Modern researchers have suggested that Teresa suffered from epilepsy, schizophrenia or some other mental disorder. Many critics in her own day insisted that she was plagued by demons. Regardless of how we evaluate Teresa's mental health today, her ability to scrutinize herself and minutely record her observations has provided us with keen insight into the dynamics of spiritual introspection that are surprisingly consistent with the results of modern psychology. Teresa is especially sensitive to the possibility of self-deception. How can she be sure that she has not put her own words into God's mouth? Teresa offers several words of advice.

First, she urges her readers not to spend lengthy periods of time alone in prayer while depressed.[21] In fact, those who suffer from "melancholy" are those most likely to mistake their own voices for God's. In the strongest of terms, Teresa urges people to ignore whatever insights seem to come to them during such bouts of despair. These people are held captive by a power beyond their control[22] and have no capacity to distinguish the genuine divine voice from their own internal accusations. We ought to ignore whatever our minds tell us during such periods of gloom.

Second, God's words, even when words of rebuke, are always spoken as "words of love (that) fill us with a love that is all-consuming."[23] Even when correcting our wrong-doing, the true voice of God will produce a sense of peace and tranquility reaffirming our Creator's desire to help and encourage, not to hate or destroy.[24]

Third, imaginary messages have no power to actually transform our lives for the better.[25] False voices will frequently leave us ill-at-ease, uncomfortable and upset, with a sense of "disquiet":[26]

> (T)his disquiet continually tortures me...it is of such a nature that one cannot discover where it comes from. The soul seems to resist it and is perturbed and afflicted without knowing why...

Notice that the anonymity of the emotional turmoil, the inability to ever pin it down, is a cardinal sign that this voice is a fraud. Such disquiet is a far cry from the tangible, positive effect that the Creator works to produce in our lives.

Fourth, and closely related to the previous point, God's message always comes with the power necessary to effect a genuine change for the better. It may not be immediate or obvious, but over time the true voice of God will work for our healing. Our God never wants to see us remain stuck in the mud. The Creator's voice will strike us as unavoidable; whereas, imaginary impressions dribble on in drips and drabs as if "someone seems to be composing bit by bit what the soul wishes to hear."[27] False voices are persistent, speaking the same message over and over again, not with the compunction of an unavoidable command, but with the eroding effect of a nagging child wearing us down until we relent.

Fifth, the spiritually sensitive person becomes more discerning over time.[28] The best way to learn to recognize God's voice is to become as familiar with God as possible. Listen. Spend time with others who are similarly attentive. Consult with friends. Teresa spent her life describing her experiences to trusted "confessors" who also relayed their own experiences and insights to her. All of her major writings were produced at the instigation of close friends who believed in the value of her experiences.

Finally, Teresa is emphatic that all messages must be measured against what we already know about God from the Old and New Testaments:[29]

> Unless it agrees strictly with the scriptures, take no more notice of it than you would if it came from the devil himself. The words may, in fact, come only from your weak imagination...

We must judge the anonymous and the disquieting by the identifiable and the reassuring. Since God has already told us in the Bible that we are immensely valued and eternally loved, any contrary voice only exposes itself as a fake.

I do not think that I need to beat my reader over the head with a lengthy discussion of the wisdom and practical value that I find in Teresa's advice. Her directives for successful mystical exploration are equally relevant for those of us wanting to distinguish God's voice from our own: never listen to the voices of depression; remember that you are infinitely loved; ignore any voice that leaves you in despair; look for God to endorse positive, life-affirming transformations; remember that experience shared with others is a most excellent teacher; and always measure your personal impressions against God's word. Teresa's principles nicely complement the lessons we have learned about guilt, shame and the distortions created by our looking-glass self. When taken together they all provide constructive guidelines for learning about oneself, coming to know the truth about God, and discerning God's real feelings towards us.

NOW THAT YOU ARE KNOWN BY GOD

The French, existentialist, philosopher Jean Paul Sartre once wrote that "I am as the Other sees me."[30] I doubt that Sartre had ever read Cooley, but the philosopher's journey led him to the same insight as Cooley had discovered through psychology. Because Sartre was an atheist, he would probably roll over in his grave to hear me say this, but he also arrived at a keen theological insight; for the ultimate Other in each of our lives is God. I am as God sees me. I am, in fact, precisely what the Creator knows me to be. This is the conclusion our study urges us to embrace.

The personal significance of this theme can be traced throughout a few of my favorite passages in the New Testament. For instance, the apostle Paul once wrote a letter to a group of friends who were seriously considering abandoning their trust in Jesus Christ. Paul wrote them a letter, now known as the New Testament book of Galatians because they lived in the Roman province of Galatia, an area stretching north and south through the midsection of Asia Minor. Paul said to them:

> In the past you did not know God...But now that you do know God—or, should I say, *now that God knows you*—how can you turn away...?

The most profound, life-altering message these ancient, spiritual seekers could ever hear was this: God knows you. It is also the most profound message any of us can hear today: God knows you. Obviously, this cannot mean that previously God had been unaware of our existence. What Paul is saying is that these men and women were, just as we are now, unconditionally, unreservedly loved as people who are fully and completely known by God. The looking-glass self may finally be shattered against the immovable rock of God's eternal love.

Another of my favorites is I Corinthians 13:12. Corinth was a thriving commercial center in what is now southern Greece. Chapter thirteen is sometimes called the love chapter because verses four through seven, extolling the self-sacrificial nature of true love, are so often included among the promises and commitments made during wedding ceremonies. However, the reading usually stops before getting to verse twelve. There we are offered a fleeting glimpse of what being perfectly known by perfect love in eternity will one day entail:

> What we see now is like a dim image in a mirror; in eternity we shall see face-to-face. What I know now is only partial; then I shall know fully, *even as I am fully known.*

To know as I am known. The promise is only as enticing as the premise. So, the question is, how well am I known? The answer: fully, completely, inside and out; there are no more secrets; no more hiding places; no more dark accusations to haunt us; no more skeletons in the closet to blackmail us into artificiality; no more reason to fear that we will one day be tracked down like Jean Valjean in *Les Misérables* and exposed for what we "really" are. Nothing about us will ever take God by surprise.

The promise, then, is that one day you and I may stand before the gates of eternal welcome where you will be received like the long-lost Prodigal. God will wrap the divine arms around your shoulders; all the archangels, the cherabim and the seraphim, will throw an intergalactic home-coming party with your name stretched across the banner of the Milky Way. In that moment of divine embrace, all the scales will fall from your eyes; the shadows that obscured so much of what you had tried to understand and accomplish will fade away as God finally pulls back the curtain on life's stage and reveals all that heaven had already known. Each piece of the puzzle will be explained. Every guilty secret will be washed away as forgiven. Unfulfilled dreams will lose their allure as they evaporate before the rising sun of all God's unexpected blessings. In a nano-second of instant, crystalline clarity, you will be made whole; you will see yourself as God had always intended you to be, and you will be content. You will know yourself as God knows you, knowing as you are known. For the rest of eternity, God's voice of unconditional acceptance is the only voice that you will hear. There will be no more distinctions between being and feeling, personhood and behavior, inside and out; there will only be one splendidly integrated you who finally knows and understands all that there is to know or understand about yourself. And what you discover is only good, simple and true.

7

ETERNAL UNION
Learning to Feel Like God

This monk can give lessons to lovers.
—Arthur Symons
quoted by Evelyn Underhill
Mysticism

I was about sixteen when I had my first experience of being imprisoned within myself. I can remember the feeling as if it happened only yesterday. I was in the middle of the Lake Washington bridge driving my parents car from Mercer Island home to north Seattle. As usual, the day was overcast; the sky was shedding a light drizzle that made the parallel iron strips in the center of the bridge as slick as axle grease. The trick to driving this part of the road was not to over-react, to simply hold the wheel steady and ignore the unsettling sensation that your car was bobbing and weaving across the lane like a punch-drunk fighter on his last legs. Somewhere in the middle of one of those weaves (or was it a bob?), I suddenly came to an uninvited perception of being utterly alone and isolated in the universe. It was an existential epiphany, a divine moment devoid of God that left me completely alone with myself.

To simply say that I felt alone makes the moment sound too pedestrian. What teenager does not feel alone even in a crowded room? But this was different. I was overwhelmed with utter and complete dread—not fear, not nerves, not anxiety about going over the edge of the bridge, but a deep, profound existential *angst* that I had never known before. It was like a drug flashback, except that I had never taken LSD. I was instantaneously transported into a parallel corridor of perception where I was able to see myself for what I really was: alone. I was trapped like *The Man in the Iron Mask*, only my condition was not the punishment of a jealous nobleman; it was my natural condition. I was trapped inside my body like a prisoner in a cage. My skull was a mask, my mouth a slit to let in air. I peered out upon the world through two, small holes. No one would ever be able to climb into this cage with me; and short of death, I would never be able to get out. My experiences were mine and mine alone; no matter how eloquently I might try to share my moods or describe my vision of the world to others, no one could truly participate in my life experience with me. We might occasionally rub noses like two rabbits in adjacent cages, but I would never really know if another's experience of a shared moment inside her cage was the same as my moment inside mine. Neither would I ever experience anyone else's view of the world with them from their perspective, and that included their perceptions of me. I cannot share my cage with you, and you cannot share your cage with me. Thus neither could I ever see myself as others saw me. Looking at myself in the mirror only offered a reversed image; a mere reflection of what others saw when they looked my way was the best I could ever hope for, assuming of course that my eyes perceived the outside world the same as everyone else's. I looked at others as they were never able to look at themselves, and others came to know me as I would never be able to know myself. What I did know of myself, no one else could ever really know, and what others knew of me, I could never know either. The entire human race was suddenly a collection of five billion isolated rabbits in five billion separate cages. In that moment of clarity, I experienced the most profound sense of absolute isolation right there in the middle of the Lake Washington bridge. It was as if I had been given an ironic gift of supernatural vision, to see reality for what it actually was. I felt detached, disconnected. It would not have mattered if my car had gone off the bridge. Those dark, choppy waters could not have felt any icier than the chill inside my skin.

That first epiphany lasted for maybe thirty seconds. It was the first but not the last. Describing the insight gleaned from that moment is like reconstructing events at the scene of a crime. There are plenty of telltale signs to indicate what probably happened, but reading the police report about a mugging is not the same as actually getting hit over the head with a gunbutt. Those are two entirely different avenues of knowledge. Throughout the years this particular mugger has snuck up behind me at the most unexpected moments causing me to relive the experience all over again. It might happen anywhere, anytime; and it did happen periodically well into my early thirties. I would suddenly become the unwilling occupant of my own skin, hermetically cut off from the people around me. The sense of isolation would last for a minute or so and then pass leaving just the faintest hint of sadness in my mouth.

HOPE IN THE GOD-MAN

Even though I never made the connection at the time, in retrospect, I believe that my isolation epiphanies began to fade as my grasp of what it means to be known by God slowly increased. Whether they were also linked in some way to the shortfall of neurochemicals in my brain, companion pieces to my eventual bouts of depression, I do not know. I do know that they subsided long before I began my relationship with Prozac. As I continued the pilgrimage of Christian faith, I learned that I was not alone after all. I had met a God who promised to inhabit my life, to indwell my cage with me and to transform me from the inside out. If this were true, then I might not have to remain alone in the world after all. First, by sharing in my life with me, I could count on God to know me at least as well if not better than I knew myself. Somebody else did know me thoroughly, inside and out, after all. More than that, my Creator might also know what was best for me. Perhaps I did not need to wander through life as if it were a cosmic, life-or-death guessing game; better yet, perhaps a personal God could offer me specific direction in a course of action that would maximize my experience of actually having something meaningful to offer the world.

Secondly, if there were others who similarly believed they too were inhabited by the same personal God who knew them as thoroughly as God knew me, then perhaps I might be able to discover a bond with them; maybe a shared experience of God could serve as a bridge between myself and other people making intimacy a real possibility. I might be able to both know and be known. Granted, it would require the faith commitment that we were sharing genuine experiences of legitimate spiritual connection; and I knew that such faith could never be the fruit of any logical proof or empirical demonstration. But after experiencing my profound isolation as a lone particle in the universe, what did I have to lose?

Finally, the Christian doctrine of the Incarnation, the belief that in Jesus of Nazareth the eternal Creator of the universe had become a human being in order to participate in every nook and cranny of my humanity, seemed to hold out a magnetic glimmer of hope that with this kind of God I could find all the necessary connections being made in my life, all the loose ends might finally be tied together.

The idea that God had once become human, had become incarnate as the Christian tradition puts it, has always staked a powerful claim upon my fascination with the Christian faith, not only intellectually but also personally. The theoretical obstacles to be overcome by such a divine-human transaction have occupied the greatest theological and philosophical minds in the history of Western civilization, and there have been long periods of time when believing in the incarnation was the norm for both great and small alike. I would not pretend to have any significant, new insights to offer in this regard. I do not understand how the immortal becomes mortal and then dies only to live again forever. How does the Creator of the universe pass through a birth canal lubricated by amniotic fluid? What does it mean for the eternal Almighty to celebrate a birthday with little brothers and sisters? God alone knows the answers to these sorts of questions. However, the intellectual inscrutability of divine behavior has never been as daunting to me as the potential for personal relevance has been attractive. I am drawn more by the hope of personal transformation than I am put off by the threat of intellectual dissatisfaction. I suppose it helps to believe, as I do, that rationality does not draw the outer boundaries on truth; reality is frequently mysterious, even inexplicable. Sometimes we may find ourselves possessed of a spiritual intuition that can lead us to a discovery the mind alone will never grasp. This does not mean that we must abandon all reason and rationality in our pursuit of spiritual truth. (I hope that this book has already made that clear). But I believe I have learned that spiritual reality is far larger than anything I can wrap my mind around.

As the ancients questioned and defended the feasibility of an incarnation, theological fallout from the discussions often provided new materials for answering a variety of related theological questions. Ironically, the idea of a God-man was used by some early, Christian thinkers to further defend the idea of divine impassibility (remember, the idea that God does not experience passion). One might suppose that an incarnation would require God to somehow join human emotions with the divine, causing God to feel genuine passion once and for all. How can the traditional doctrine of impassibility ever be squared with the Christian belief in the incarnation? After all, the New Testament makes it clear that Jesus experienced emotion just like any other human being. He is reported to have been angry, disappointed, happy, sad, content, disillusioned and depressed. If the God-man felt passion, doesn't that mean that God now has first-hand knowledge of the ups and downs of emotional travail, at least from the human, temporal side of the equation if not from the divine eternal?

Actually, we have already encountered one ancient solution to that problem, and even though you may not initially care about rummaging around in theological libraries or answering such religious conundrums yourself, I hope to show that finding a good answer to this particular question is ultimately to find an answer to our most pressing personal quest for love and emotional well-being. It has always been important for the Christian church to affirm that, as God in the flesh, the incarnate Son of God possessed two natures simultaneously. There was a divine nature and a human nature cohabiting in the one God-man, Jesus. Conveniently, for advocates of impassiblity, the human nature participated in such human experiences as emotion, while the divine nature—in order to remain fully divine—continued unscathed by such inappropriate human experiences. Remember that Clement of Alexandria made full use of this explanation: Christ suffered in his humanity but remained unchanged in his divinity; since emotion requires change, the divine nature never experienced emotion (see chapter one). This has been a common assertion throughout the history of Christian theology. However, as you might have guessed, it is an answer I find completely unsatisfying. Fortunately, I am not alone. A brilliant, fourth-century leader of the Egyptian church named Athanasius would have also taken issue with Clement's solution, and even though he might not fully approve of my own position or my use of his thinking, Athanasius' discussion of what it means for Jesus to be the God-man provides me with the hope to believe that not only does God fully understand my emotional life, but Jesus provides me with the greatest prospect of complete, eventual emotional healing.

AN EGYPTIAN BEST-SELLER

Believe it or not, Jackie Collins did not invent the best-selling, celebrity biography. All throughout history, from Plato's reminiscences about the death of Socrates to the contemporary fascination with Princess Diana, the well-written story of an unusual or exemplary life has been used both to motivate and to educate the reading public. In A.D. 356 the leader of the Christian church in Egypt published the biography of a locally known, desert hermit that not only influenced the course of church history but continues to be reprinted and read to this day. The monk's name was Antony. The author was Athanasius of Alexandria (A.D. 295-373). Almost as soon as it was written, *The Life of Antony* was translated from Greek into Latin (for a western readership) and Coptic (for the eastern common-folk) becoming an international best-seller throughout the Byzantine empire.

Athanasius was a successor to the great Alexandrian theologians Clement and Origen, responsible for leading the Christian church throughout Egypt as well as the theological academy resident in the capital, Alexandria. Athanasius, however, was cut from a different bolt of cloth than his predecessors. He has been called a "supreme churchman," the first Egyptian bishop to preach in the Coptic venacular of his uneducated parishioners. He shirked the label of theologian and preferred to be seen as a pastor who cared more about the spiritual health of his flock than the theological sophistication of his last treatise. The task of good theology, according to Athanasius, was to build up the church and provide a solid basis for the believer's earthly hopes and eternal aspirations. Tenacious and defiantly devoted to the fortunes of the Christian church, he was not above publicly defying the emporer if he believed that defending the integrity of the church required it; in fact, he was exiled five times by the powers-that-be with more than one plot set in motion to have him thrown into an unmarked grave in the Egyptian wilderness.

Even though Athanasius was an intellectual giant, he did not feel particularly at home in the classical, philosophical tradition of his predecessors having a greater affinity for the Old and New Testaments than the writings of Greek philosophy. A prolific author, he was nevertheless a leader of men before he was a writer of books. One historian has described him as "the first Greek Father who did not regard himself as a Christian philosopher"[1]—a supremely ironic description given the fact that his theological writings eventually set the standard for orthodox, Christian teaching in both the east and west. One sixth century abbott told a young novice that "if you find something of the writings of St. Athanasius and you have no paper handy, write it on your clothes."[2]

The scorched sands of the Egyptian interior had attracted lone, holy men seeking spiritual purification since at least the second century A.D. Driven by a desire to see God that was channeled through the hellenistic impulse to free oneself from life's material trappings, they ecked out a hard-scrabble existence in caves and stone lean-tos dotted throughout an inhospitable wilderness. It did not take long before stories began to circulate about desert saints who spoke with God face to face, successfully wrestled with the devil himself, and shared their visions of heaven with any spiritual seeker who humbly sought them out looking for a word from the Lord.

Antony was hardly the first of these desert mystics, but Athanasius' treatment of his life would help to create a new movement of desert communities formed by spiritual devotees, men and women alike, willing to do whatever was required to experience peace and harmony with their Creator. Antony's parents died when he was around twenty years old leaving him in charge of a younger sister and a large estate. Entering a church service one afternoon, he heard the gospel reading, "If you want to be perfect, go, sell what you possess and give to the poor, and you will have treasure in heaven."[3] Gripped by the voice of God, that is exactly what he did. After selling all his inheritance and arranging for his sister to be cared for by the virgins in a local convent, Antony moved into the desert. By the time he died, Antony had become a legendary figure exerting more influence from his desert cave than many a bishop from his plush headquarters. Athanasius described him as the perfect reflection of physical and spiritual well-being, a happy integration of mind, will and emotion into the loving, contented disposition God originally intended for us all. The key to this personal transformation was not only the ascetic practices of self-denial and extreme discipline, but, perhaps even more importantly, Antony's faith in the incarnation of Christ. You see, Athanasius was something of a propogandist as well as a theologian. He knew how to communicate with the masses; this best-selling biography not only told a crackin' good story about a local hero, but did so by promoting the key issues of Athanasius' own theology. For, at that time, Athanasius was one of the chief protagonists in an unresolved, critical contest to establish the eternal deity of Christ as an essential factor in Christian salvation. If Christ was not truly divine, he insisted, then he could not truly save. Antony, a representative of this position himself—at least, as portrayed in *The Life*—became an influential, popular apologist for the life transforming power of faith in the true God-man, Jesus Christ. As the eighty year old monk prepared for death, his visitors marvelled at his unusually good health and disposition. He even had all his teeth (!), a rare sight in those days and an obvious indication of profound spirituality:[4]

> His soul being free of confusion, he held his outer senses also undisturbed, so that from the soul's joy his face was cheerful as well, and from the movements of the body it was possible to sense and to perceive that stable condition of the soul...for he was never troubled, his soul being calm, and he never looked gloomy, his mind being filled with joy.

Athanasius' point is that by coming to know God through Christ, Antony had learned to know himself through Christ, and the vision of being wholly engulfed by Christ's perfect humanity burned away all confusion, doubt and discontent. Having originally been created as God's good creature, faith in Jesus now allows the divinely intended individual to emerge whole and complete. By loving Christ, the self-contradictions and emotional turmoil of Antony's natural self were melted away:[5]

> Virtue is not far from us, nor does it stand external to us, but its realization lies within us . . . For virtue . . . holds fast according to its nature when it remains as it was made—and it was made beautiful and perfectly straight.

The "real you" is waiting to emerge in brilliant transparency like a butterfly breaking free from its cocoon. Your genuine identity lies hidden, obscured by a lifetime of misunderstanding, guarded by numerous defense mechanisms; but Christ's love waits to call you out of yourself, to peal away the accumulated layers of sinful residue, and to remake you as God has always intended you to be. This is the "virtue" inherent within each of us, placed there by our Creator.

How does this process of self-discovery take place? What role does the God-man have to play?

GROWING UP TO BE LIKE GOD

What little child does not want to grow up to be like mom or dad? There is nothing that our parents cannot seem to do when we are young. As a ten year old ruffian hanging out in the neighborhood carports, I once accosted a teenager with a golf bag slung over his shoulder. My father had recently taken up golf, so without knowing anything about the game, I asked, "Do you play golf?"

"Sure do."

"Oh yea? My dad golfs."

"Good for him."

I could tell that he was not sufficiently impressed. Forging ahead I asked, "How well do you golf?"

"Oh, about 110," he replied.

He was mine. "Hah," I shouted. "That's nothin'. My dad golfs about 500!"

It was a long time before I understood why he walked away laughing.

I wanted to grown up to be like my dad. He rode horses, so I wanted to ride horses. He enjoyed sailboats, so I wanted to learn to sail. He was a career Army officer, so I planned to voluteer for Viet Nam—something he convinced me not to do. Even those areas which remained less attractive exerted their influence over the years; I too can be withdrawn and uncommunicative at times. There was a genetic seed planted at conception that has developed under the influence of my environment and unbringing to permanently mark me as a member of the Crump family. Not even the adolescent about-face that one day found me swearing I would never be like my father could erase the multitude of unforeseen ways in which I was destined to become very much like him.

Good parents give themselves to their children, and more children grow up to be like their parents than are willing to admit it. The genius of Athanasius was his recognition that the New Testament teaching on the incarnation places this very metaphor center-stage in the Christian view of salvation. In his most important work, *On the Incarnation of the Word of God*, Athanasius boldly asserts:[6]

> He became human that we might be made God!

As shocking as this may sound to some, it is a conviction that has been repeated many times by leading figures throughout Christian history. Irenaeus, Clement of Alexandria, Origen and Augustine, for example, all made similar if not identical statements in their own writings.[7] Yet nobody staked as much upon the meaning of that sentence as Athanasius. He called it "deification" or "divinization"—the Christian's opportunity to become like God. However, it is important to clarify for the modern reader that none of these men actually expected to become essentially divine; we do not join the pantheon. Deification language is a rhetorical attempt to convey the radical significance of the spiritual transformation that engulfs us once we place our faith in Christ; the change is so dramatic that we do become as "god-like" as it is possible for humanity to become. God is that generous. However, in keeping with New Testament teaching, Athanasius also regularly highlights two essential distinctions between the deity of Christ and the deification of humanity. Christ is (1) the eternal Creator who is (2) divine by nature. We, on the other hand, are (1) creatures who (2) become "divine" by adoption.[8] Our divinity is not the same as God's, but is the excessively generous gift of a Creator who works to share all that can possibly be shared with the creation.

Origen was the first to coin the term "God-man" in reference to Christ.[9] Not only did this One, known as the eternal Word, come to reveal the fullness of God in human history, but he also exemplified the real flesh and blood possibility of the human spirit being united with the divine. The incarnation of God-come-in-the-flesh was the restoration of that original unity intended by the Creator between mortal and immortal; that baby's birth in a manger was the downpayment of "the redeification" of the entire spiritual and physical realm.[10]

Earlier Irenaeus had taught something very similar that has come to be called "recapitulation."[11] That is, the salvation made available to us through Jesus Christ is the result of his successfully living the perfect, human existence that God had always wished for each of us, including our first mother and father. Where we have failed, Christ succeeds. Jesus of Nazareth offered God a life of perfect, human love on our behalf, so that through faith, we might receive a perfect, spiritual existence with God. According to both recapitulation and deification, salvation is not only the result of Christ's death on the cross but flows to us from the entire experience of his life on earth. Death and resurrection may have been the pinnacle of Jesus' obedience, but qualitatively those events were no different from a hundred and one other acts of self-surrender offered up to the Creator as he walked through ancient Galilee.

One New Testament source for this line of theological reflection, which may have influenced the thinkers mentioned above, is found in the New Testament letter called Second Peter, chapter one, verse four:

> God has given us the very great and precious gifts he promised, so that by means of these gifts you may escape from the

destructive forces in this world, and *come to share in the divine nature.*

To share in the divine nature, to become divine (so to speak), this is the central ingredient in Athanasius' hope for the world. Our incorporation into Christ by faith transports us from our current fragmentation and brokenness to be integrated into God's own spiritual perfection. Jesus' own perfect humanity becomes ours; and as perfect human beings we simultaneously become perfect, spiritual children of God.

DEIFICATION

I grew up wanting to be Jimmy Page, one of the greatest rock and roll guitar players of all time. I had studied the guitar for a dozen years as a child and, at one time or another, had applied myself to a wide variety of styles from classical to pop, "The Red River Valley" to "Jumpin' Jack Flash." But try as I might, there was one thing I could never do. I was never able to improvise the music I heard in my head; in fact, I rarely heard music in my head at all. I could replay somebody else's music, sometimes even with dexterity and panache, but I could never really jam. I was incapable of joining other musicians and simply making music happen spontaneously in the moment. And if I could not jam, I could never be Jimmy Page, or Eric Clapton, or Jeff Beck. It did not matter if I went to a concert, watched their fingers from the front row, and then returned home to precisely reproduce what I had seen them do on stage. I could never participate in the musical moment myself, and there is a big difference between the two. After years of frustration, I finally reconciled myself to the fact that I could study the guitar for the rest of my life, and I would never overcome that particular musical limitation.

Motivational speakers are fond of telling us that if we will only discipline ourselves to never abandon the pursuit of our dreams, we can eventually do anything and become anyone we want. Don't believe it. The motivational rhetoric regurgitated for us as children simply is not true. I cannot do anything or be anyone I want simply because that is what I want, and neither can you. It certainly is true that too many of us settle for second-best. We often stop far short of our potential because we quit much too soon. But there are some things in life I will never be able to do, no matter how hard I try, because success is not simply a function of effort, modelling, or attitude; it depends heavily upon raw ability. In fact, ability is fundamental. Drape a positive, mental attitude around a woman who is tone deaf, and all you will ever have is an unrealistic singer who regularly embarrasses herself in public. Before I would ever play like Jimmy or Eric, I first needed a mystical transfusion of their ability; the spirit of the guitar gods would need to draw from the well of musical soul and anoint me with heavy metal thunder that would burn deep within and erupt in flashes of brilliance through my fingertips. Then and only then would all my hours of practice be able to transform my boyhood dreams into reality. It never happened.

In my quest for spiritual integration, I need a similar transfusion of supernatural ability if I ever hope to reach the imagined depths of contentment for which I search. I want to be suffused with peace and tranquility, but they continue to elude me no matter how hard I try. I yearn to make connection with divine love but do not know where to find it. I need healing for my emotional fragmentation but do not even know the source of my confusion, much less where to find the answers to my questions. We all require a spiritual rescue arising from some source outside of ourselves. Athanasius insists that Jesus Christ is the solution we seek, not simply because he loves us, or forgives us, or wishes us well. Although each of these offers is certainly true, they are all gifts that can be given from a distance. However, as the God-man, Christ has accomplished three crucial acheivements that bring him closer to me than I am to myself:

First, he has participated in my humanity. The divine Word—the designation Athanasius uses for the pre-incarnate Christ—became a real, time-bound human being. God did not put on humanity in the way an astronaut wears a space suit; God was not simply using Jesus' body to perform an "earth walk." No. Somehow, God became human such that the entire human experience (with the exception of disobedience) became God's experience. However we may want to finally answer the "two natures" question, there was only *one person* experiencing the full life of Jesus of Nazareth. That one flesh and blood person, simultaneously both fully God and fully human, grew hungry and thirsty, became tired and discouraged as well as optimistic and joyful, knew sadness and suffering, wept, groaned and finally suffocated during execution upon a Roman cross. According to Athanasius, in this way God really did experience the full range of human emotion:[12]

> The Word bore the infirmities of the flesh as His own, for the flesh was His...The Godhead was in it, for the body was God's.
>
> He had a body, not in appearance, but in truth; and it was proper for the Lord, in putting on human flesh, to put it on completely with the affections proper to it...

We see that Athanasius soundly rejected Clement's formula for delivering Christ the God-man from experiencing the passions of human suffering and emotion. Athanasius would not split Jesus down the middle and say that the human half knew suffering while the divine half remained immune to pain. That kind of savior could never have provided the wholistic deliverance humanity required. Athanasius rightly insisted that "what was not assumed could not be redeemed." In other words, in order to heal our emotional lives, Christ first needed to take human emotions into the Godhead. We all need to know that, regardless of our circumstances, God empathizes with us; God understands because the Creator has joined hands with each of us in the nitty-gritty details of our mundane existence. Our aches and pains, disappointments and frustrations are not foreign to God after all, not since Jesus came.

Second, Athanasius highlights that whatever degree of empathy is made possible by Christ's incarnation, by remaining wholly God, the God-man also retains the unique ability to *literally* share in my life experience with me. Christ is more than a sympathetic friend who has walked this road before; he is also the indwelling God who now walks my road with me. When Jesus received the gift of the Holy Spirit, he was filled with the power of God on my behalf, thereby creating my own potential "receptivity" to the Spirit.[13] Because He was filled with the Spirit, the same miracle-working power that allowed Jesus to heal the sick and cause the blind to see is now activated within me.

Consequently, I am no longer alone in my rabbit cage; the Spirit of God lives within me. Christ now sees all that I see exactly as I can see it. But more than that, as my Creator, Christ can also work to correct my misperceptions teaching me where, when and how I see things inaccurately. This includes correcting the ways in which I view myself. I may not be able to climb out of my skin to see myself as others see me, but I can learn to see myself as God sees me, discovering that the Creator knows me as I was meant to be. God views my potential as if it were actual and then supernaturally leads me towards its fulfilment. By learning to see through the eyes of this indwelling God, I can walk life's high-road exploring the supernatural opportunities to which I might otherwise be blind.

A sensitive, loving parent looks beyond a child's failures and mistakes to see her potential. Mothers and fathers invest for the long-term. Many of the most successful people you will ever meet are the ones who can stand up and say, "My parents never stopped believing in me." Similarly, by working to transform us from the inside out, God focuses upon what we can be, not simply what we are. Thus by following God's direction I continue to reside in my bodily cage, but it is no longer my cell. I am an individual but never isolated. God now sends me aerial photos of my place in the world, and connects me to a network of fellow travelers while leading me towards my perfect future.

Before finishing with this theme of participation, we must make one more crucial observation. Athanasius' insistence upon Christ's assumption of human emotions produces an unavoidable paradox, and we will not properly understand the healing prospects offered in the incarnation if we fail to grasp its significance. God did not become any less God by becoming human. Yet, this creates quite a conundrum for Athanasius, since he continues to be a man of his age in wanting simultaneously (and paradoxically) to insist upon the traditional notion of divine impassibility. In other words, insofar as he was God, Christ did not experience human emotions after all:[14]

> The Word is impassible by nature, and yet because of that flesh which He put on, things (such as suffering) are ascribed to Him since they are proper to the flesh...(B)eing impassible in nature, the Saviour remains as He is, not harmed by these affections...

In other words, as both created human and eternal God, Christ was passible and impassible, suffered and did not suffer, experienced emotion and did not experience emotion, all at the same time. Clement had tried to avoid this paradox by saying that whereas Christ's body suffered, the Word did not. Athanasius, on the other hand, embraces the conundrum whole:[15]

> It is a truly wonderful paradox that He suffered and did not suffer. He suffered because his own body suffered...Yet he did not suffer because the Word, being by nature God, is impassible.

Though the modern, scientific mind may be inclined to simply dismiss this conundrum as nonsensical, it would be a mistake for us to be intellectually smug. For not only is Athanasius quite conscious of the paradox, "he considers it to be intrinsic" to the promise of salvation;[16] it pulses at the heart of our prospects for deification, as he put it.

Christ's final accomplishment was to make us like God. Once God had become human, a way was finally created for humanity to enter into the divine. Although we cannot forget that deification is spelled with a small "d," Athanasius, no stranger to controversy, provocatively insists upon the full measure of its implications:

> The Word assumed humanity that we might become God... He endured shame that we might inherit immortality.[17]

> The Word became flesh that humanity might be capable of Godhead.[18]

> The Lord, putting on the body, became human, so we are deified by the Word as being taken into Him through His flesh, and from now on, we inherit eternal life.[19]

Through the incarnation a cosmic transaction has taken place that makes the impossible possible, redeems it and transforms it into a new, spiritual reality given to humanity. We may now attain to the divine:[20]

> Who will not agree that such a thing is truly divine? For if the works of the Word's Godhead had not taken place through the

body, humanity would not have been deified; and again, had not the properties of the flesh been ascribed to the Word, humanity would not have been thoroughly delivered from them...

Since Christ assumed every feature of our humanity, all of our humanity (including our emotions) is now transformed, recreated. We are no longer simply human in the familiar sense—as stumbling, finite creatures second-guessing our way through life's confusion. We become human in a new sense, a sense new to us but not to God—as perfect bearers of the divine image created to be God's own beloved companions. Athanasius uses the language of deification to shock us into accepting the incomprehensible, spiritual transformation now available in Christ. The paradox of the God-man, so flagrantly embraced by Athanasius, is also central to the paradox of our own deification. Whereas, through Christ we may become divine (that is, *perfectly* human), we never forget that even with Christ we are not the same as God. Christ's paradox arose from the fact that the Word took on humanity while remaining intrinsically deity. Our paradox results from the correlary—we are creatures deified by adoption through God's grace.[21]

Reality is woven together by a network of divine connections so that when God pulled upon the lone thread named Jesus of Nazareth two thousand years ago, the entire fabric of time and space was pulled along after him. When Jesus entered into his resurrection glory, the whole universe—from the single-cell amoeba to the vast, undiscovered nebula in darkest space—was simultaneously engulfed by eternal light. Christ dove into creation's web and carried the cosmos into his perfection restoring what we were always intended to be: divine companions to the Divine.

SHARING IN GOD'S EMOTIONS

Old habits die hard. Traditional theology, even when flawed, dies harder. Athanasius believed he needed to adhere to the Alexandrian tradition asserting God's impassibility. This was no particular problem since impassibility alone was not the substance of the incarnational paradox; it was merely one (non-essential) feature among others that were crucial. However, it did have a telling consequence for

Athanasius' view of Christian spirituality. The deified believer, in approaching union with the impassible God, would find her own passions burned away. Athanasius' portrait of Antony offers his ideal of such a dispassionate saint, immune to all disturbance, never deflected from his joyful contemplation of the divine. At this point, we should recall that the Greek tradition did not define passion as any and all emotion, but as the uncontrolled emotional disturbance that distracted one from the proper focus upon God's will for one's life. Perhaps we might compare passion to substance abuse. Enjoying alcohol in moderation is one thing, but organizing your life around happy-hour is quite another. Like alcoholism, the passions hijack your life and take you to places a sensible person would never go. Passion is not just feeling *per se* but counter-productive feeling. Remember that Antony is described as feeling calm and joyful as he faces death. Nevertheless, having said this, if we can legitimately eliminate the superfluous commitment to impassibility on other grounds, we are free to explore a far broader horizon for developing the emotional potential of our deified union with the Creator. By being united in relationship with God and finding the personal virtues implanted within us by the Spirit, we are now given the prospects of complete emotional, even passionate, well-being. Set free from the crippling effects of our separation from the Creator, our emotions are liberated to become what God always intended them to be: finite echoes of the infinite, eternal heart. Now we may possibly experience self-giving love free of any smothering possessiveness; appropriate jealousy with no hint of selfish envy; necessary sadness that never bleeds into despair because it knows that any setback is only temporary; righteous anger purified of all bitterness and revenge as we patiently await God's solution; and joy that elevates the senses, both physical and spiritual, whether derived from the tiniest, quixotic coincidence or the long-awaited fulfilment of a dream. By attending to a personal relationship with Jesus Christ, we may come to know ourselves as we are known by God, integrated, whole, complete.

At least I know that this is how I have experienced Christ's work in my life. For example, when I first began dating my young wife-to-be I was a relational pigmy, to put it mildly. It was still very early days in my life with God and, being the solemn loner that I was, interpersonal communication had never been my strong suit. My average conversation consisted of a grunt followed by a cough. Yet, as a college sophomore two new influences began to permanently reshape my character and personality. First, I had hooked up with a group of fellow students who were all equally committed to exploring their relationships with God; and, second, I had begun to fall in love with a young woman who truly wanted to know me and was willing to invest whatever time was necessary in helping a clumsy young man, completely out of touch with who he was, begin to express his feelings and to see the world in brand new ways. Terry and I would sometimes take long walks together where I would struggle for what seemed like hours to haltingly mutter disjointed stabs at self-expression. She was always patient and understanding, willing to wait for as long at took as I fumbled to find the right syllables, often not even sure of what I was trying to say. Such personal communication was virgin terrain to me; I had never opened myself so completely to anyone before. Yet, despite the occasional pain and embarrassment of the effort involved, I was magnetically drawn outside of myself because I knew that I was coming to be known by someone very special. The more I opened up, the deeper the intimacy and the more I was known. The more I was known, the more alive the rest of my emotions became; in fact, parts of my emotional life began to bloom that I never even knew I had.

My emotional coming of age was occurring within a larger context. I was also seriously trying to apply myself to understanding more about God's work and availability in my life. Although it was only a faint intuition at the time, I can now see that the lessons I was learning about personal intimacy were running parallel to the lessons I was being taught by God; in fact, they were deeply intertwined. My interactions with Terry were teaching me about the grace of God, and my growth with God was a significant factor enabling me to become transparent with Terry. This was the period of my life when I first began to experience what it meant for God to love me just as I was. God knew me, knew everything there was to know about me, just as Terry loved me more as she learned more about me. Her love was not a necessary result of this knowledge; actually, anyone else might have been driven away by some of the secrets I had to share. Sometimes I suspected she loved me inspite of the things she learned. But she loved me as God loved me, and God was loving me in her love. And in this hot-house of unconditional love, my emotions began to swell. I started to learn how to cry without being ashamed; how to be fearful without embarrassment; how to disagree without the paralysis of insecurity; how to let go of my cynicism in order to embrace new hope. I was learning to feel like God.

LEARNING TO BE KNOWN

As you may have gathered already, the key to this healing process is to focus upon the dynamics of *being known* as opposed to merely *knowing*. As Abraham Heschel has said, "This is the task: to sense or to discover our being known. We approach (God), not by making (the divine) the object of our thinking, but by discovering ourselves as the objects of (God's) thinking."[22] We are transformed as we surrender ourselves to, and even learn to delight in, God's tender invasion of our lives. Consider these contrasts:

- knowing oneself vs. being known by another
- mastery vs. cooperation
- the mind vs. the heart
- independence vs. connectedness

First, knowledge by itself can do nothing to solve the problems of isolation. Just think of how quiet the local library can be, filled with so many people and so little communication. Everyone is studying to know more, but no one knows what anyone else is learning. This kind of study by itself will never provide many of the lessons we most desperately need. Lessons such as how to make another person smile. How to calm a friend's fears. How to say "I love you" in a language the beloved can hear. Remaining perpetually focused upon oneself is like reading a book alone in the library. You may learn a lot through research (as in therapy or counselling), but whenever we concentrate upon simply gaining knowledge for ourselves, we are locked into a very limiting process. Ironically, simply coming to know—whether it is the knowledge of facts, of myself, or even of another person—is never as enriching as simultaneously being known. To know *of* another does not necessarily require her presence in my live. However, to be known *by* another means that I am personally present to her. To be known opens up the doorway to relationship and mutual understanding. I am no longer isolated; I have a companion who is interested in exploring who I am. I can easily look at someone else and say, "I know who you are" without feeling any type of personal connection whatsoever. But to say to another, "You really know me" is to conjure an intimacy never acquired through books in a study hall.

Secondly, to be known means that I can no longer be the lone sovereign of my personal life. Now I must learn to cooperate by divesting myself of the need to be in complete control and by offering myself to the other as someone who wants to be known. This process always involves risk. Will they like what they learn about me? Will I be willing to change should they ask as someone whose friendship I have come to value? When I simply come to know, I remain the master of my intellectual conquests. After all, aren't we told that information is power? I come to know so-and-so or such-and-such by my own efforts; knowledge is my accomplishment. In some respects, for me to know you is even to have a certain measure of power over you; I may try to use what I know to manipulate you, to gain the upper hand in our relationship. But once I learn to cooperate in the process of being known, I also discover that I must surrender my need for control. Rather, I must listen attentively and respond to what you may desire without any control over the possible consequences. I learn to trust, to become vulnerable, to have faith, to open myself up to new possibilities, possibilities largely determined by someone else.

Thirdly, it is entirely possible for the learning process to engage nothing more than the mind. I can easily come to know you without actually knowing the first thing *about* you. How often have we been shocked to learn that the neighbors we have "known" for 20 years are suddenly getting a divorce, and yet no one ever suspected that anything was wrong? We might say that we knew them; but if asked, I suspect that the divorcing couple would reply that no one really knew them at all. To be known requires full engagement, emotional and intellectual. I want to be known for who I am, so I gingerly begin to open up my hidden recesses to another's searching eye. If I do not, I will never be known. The other, as an eager investigator, receives what I have to give regardless of its size or shape, and a little bit more of my inner life has been accepted. This type of self-disclosure necessarily involves the heart because it touches upon our secret places. It is no surprise, then, to learn that marriages embedded within support networks, where their struggles are known and understood by others who care for them, have a better chance of finding healing and reconciliation than couples who struggle by themselves.

Finally, being genuinely known rings the death knell for our stubborn independence. People who insist upon keeping to themselves are never truly known by anyone. They seldom even know themselves. To be known by someone else is to become enmeshed in personal relationships where I am often reflected back to myself. When I make myself transparent to another, new pathways of connection are forged between the two of us. We are no longer isolated by our rabbit cages. I am known by you, and you are known by me. Our secrets are no longer ours alone.

Christ's intrusion into our world has ensured that we will forever be thoroughly known by the God who loves us, secrets and all. Each of the factors involved in being known by others are equally important to that relationship. In fact, the human dynamic is derived from the divine. Surrendering our need to be in control, moving beyond the intellect to the engagement of our entire being, becoming part of a community of shared faith, and honestly yielding ourselves to the consequences of intimacy with God, these are all crucial ingredients in seeing our new divine life take root and mature.

Perhaps it is summarized best in the language of surrender.

We must surrender ourselves to Christ. We surrender as those who are already most intimately and profoundly known. Though we know so very little ourselves, we accept that we are exhaustively known by God. We surrender to the fact that there are no more secrets, no more hiding places. We simply stop trying to get away.

We surrender to seeking connection with other like-minded searchers. By allowing ourselves to become known to others, we will be introduced to new avenues of emotional discovery.

We finally surrender to God's control. Our compulsion to control consigns us to permanent emotional atrophy. By risking faith in

God's loving power over our lives, we begin a life-long adventure of becoming ourselves by becoming like Christ.

Only those who surrender will discover what it means to finally feel like God.

8

A LONG AND WINDING ROAD

Sustaining Faith for the Journey

Only when the single individual turns inward into himself . . .
does he become aware and capable of seeing God . . .
It is really the God-relationship that makes
a human being a human being.
— Søren Kierkegaard
Concluding Unscientific Postscript

We have made a long journey together and covered a lot of foreign ground, not all of it easily travelled. Hopefully, you have made it this far without skinning your spiritual knees too often—although a tumble now and again is to be expected on any long trip, and the occasional stubbed toe is easily forgotten, especially if you know you are making progress towards a worthwhile destination. The difference between taking a family vacation and making a spiritual pilgrimage (aside from the obvious) is that the first usually makes use of a map, whereas the second begins with nothing more than a goal. You see, there are no maps for spiritual journeys. There are stories, descriptions, legends and various sorts of directions handed down through the generations, but no maps exist for such ventures as spiritual awakening. God is not a pot of gold at the end of the rainbow, and no two spiritual journey are exactly alike. The best one can hope for is a good compass, yet as long as the compass always points true north that is all you really need. If you already know where you want to go, the compass will keep you headed in the right direction. But we both know that is a very big "if" and the chief stumbling block for many.

A compass cannot direct you to any particular route, but it can show you which way to start walking. The difficulty with following a compass rather than a map is that we are very impatient people. Most of us want a detailed plan for the entire course of our lives that will precisely plot our progress each step of the way, not only for family vacations but for life-long spiritual journeys as well. I want to know in advance how long it will take, how much further I have to go, what is coming up at the next stop, how to avoid possible obstacles and when to take whatever shortcuts I need for a speedy arrival. It can take a long time to outgrow the youthful "are we there yet?" frame of mind. Controlling our spiritual impatience is something we each must learn for ourselves, but it does become easier with time and progress.

I have tried to provide a spiritual compass that will keep us heading in the right direction as we continue in our quest for intimacy with God. This particular compass will always keep Jesus the God-man in our immediate line of sight. No one can foresee the specifics of their journey or the twists and turns that lay ahead; different travelers will choose divergent paths. My difficulties will not be the same as yours; my baggage was packed by a different household. No one is required to follow in anyone else's footsteps, and we could not do it even if we tried. However, as long as we continue to progress towards Christ, we can know that we are on the right track getting closer to our final goal, our true home. In fact, we may well find ourselves strangely empowered at times by a new, motivating force as we draw nearer to this God-man; the closer we come, the more powerfully we are attracted, until we occasionally find ourselves being lifted, elevated and drawn irresistibly by a magnetic, spiritual force identifying itself as divine love. Eventually, the Spirit of God will personally ferry us over potential pitfalls and snares in the divine arms moving us ahead with an impetus and conviction more powerful than anything we could muster on our own.

We began our journey by investigating the possibility of God's possessing a real emotional life. In affirming that divine emotions are genuine, eternal passions that reach out and engage each of us in personal relationship, we were inevitably led to the traditional notion of humanity's creation in the image of God, which elicited a crucial conclusion: human passions are actually a distorted reflection of God's original, emotional intent for humanity. God's plan was that my emotional life be a harmonious reflection of the divine emotions; that my passions would intertwine with the divine affections just as the divine would commingle with and sustain my own interior life. With this hope before us, we eventually concluded our journey by discovering that the incarnation of Jesus Christ has made it possible for us to become perfected, healed and reconstituted as the emotionally whole people we were created to be. Healing and reintegration are eventual certainties as we find ourselves introduced by faith into the Godhead through the incarnation of Christ.

Incidentally, we have also discovered that, while our progress depends upon faith, such faith is not without its own substantive signs of encouragement along the way. Like the proverbial bread crumbs strewn along the trail, we have regularly come across the odd bits of evidence—whether from biology, sociology, psychology or anthropology—that are entirely commensurate with this Judaeo-Christian tradition (at least, as represented by Tertullian, Athanasius and others of their ilk). We do need faith for the journey, but it is not a blind, irrational faith; in fact, the further we advance, the more sensible such faith seems to become. After all, the proof of the pudding is in the eating, and this particular pudding (forgive the mixed metaphors) provides all the energy needed for us to maintain progress. Emotional healing offers reason enough to accept the sensibility of such faith.

We have learned that the classic, Greek distinction between being and becoming has severely misdirected the historic quest for God. Despite its overwhelming popularity throughout the ages, that particular compass has never pointed true north. The Old and New Testaments portray a God of supreme pathos engaged in a network of real-time relationships animated by emotional give and take. This is how God and the individual together write a lifestory. History's plotline is not about individuals *becoming* on their way to divine *Being*; it is about eternal *Concern* reaching out for personal *relationship* and subsuming us in the divine embrace. True spirituality surrenders to the knowledge that our experience of God is always God's prior experience of us.

There is also plenty of evidence that earlier, wiser pilgrims have gone this way before. True, there are no maps, but over time enough eager seekers have employed the same compass that history's landscape is strewn with the hand-carved sign posts and personalized messages left behind by our predecessors encouraging us not to give up. Their testimonies of eventual union with God and emotional harmony may help us to sustain our quest. Such saints as Antony and Teresa assure us that emotional well-being is not only possible but genuinely available to us in Christ—the God who knows us better than we know ourselves; the God who feels for us more deeply than we have ever felt. One day, as we use this compass to pursue our journey, we will finally learn to feel as we were meant to feel and to know as we have always been known.

NOTES

CHAPTER 1

[1] I deliberately have avoided the term "fundamentalist" in my description. The phenomenon I describe is much broader than that typically encompassed by this term; furthermore, the word has become so misused that it can have little descriptive value in a discussion such as ours.

[2] Text in J. Stevenson, ed. *Creeds, Councils and Controversies* (London: SPCK, 1966), p. 336; quoted in Paul Fiddes, *The Creative Suffering of God*, (Oxford: Clarendon Press, 1988), p. 1.

[3] Bellarmino Bagatti, *The Church from the Circumcision: History and Archaeology of the Judaeo-Christians* (Jerusalem: Franciscan Printing Press, 1971), pp. 86-87. After examining the lists of those in attendance, Bagatti concludes that not one Jewish Christian attended the Council of Nicaea in 325 A.D., the first important ecumenical council addressing the doctrine of God. For controversy over the use of biblical vs. non-biblical vocabulary in the early theological debates see, R. P. C. Hanson, *The Search for the Christian Doctrine of God: the Arian Controversy, 318-381* (Edinburgh: T. & T. Clark, 1988), pp. 167, 192, 205, 422.

[4] See Joseph McLelland, *God the Anonymous: A Study in Alexandrian Philosophical Theology* (Cambridge, MA: Philadelphia Patristic Foundation: 1976), p. 162. McLelland suggests that modern ways of thinking such as "rationalism" and "empiricism" are best described as "philosophies of revolt against theism...They reflect the logical extension of the *deus absolutus* and his remoteness from the created order..."

[5] (New York: Harper & Row, 1967), pp. 257, 260; emphasis mine. See the helpful discussion of the development of philosophical atheism as the revolt

against the God of metaphysics in Brian Ingraffia, *Postmodern Theory and Biblical Theology* (Cambridge: Cambridge University Press, 1995).

[6] *Phaedo*, 78a-83b; *Great Dialogues of Plato* (Trans. by W. H. D. Rouse; New York: Mentor Books, 1956), pp. 483-488.

[7] *Symposium*, 211c; quoted from *Great Dialogues of Plato*, p. 105.

[8] I refer to the Penguin Classics edition, *Timaeus and Critias* (Trans. by Desmond Lee; New York: Penguin Books, 1965). For the theological influence of the *Timaeus* among both Jewish and Christian thinkers see David Runia, *Philo of Alexandria and the Timaeus of Plato* (Leiden: E. J. Brill, 1986); Jaroslav Pelikan, *What Has Athens to Do with Jerusalem? Timaeus and Genesis in Counterpoint* (Ann Arbor: University of Michigan Press, 1997).

[9] 28a.

[10] 38a.

[11] 28c.

[12] *Timaeus* 28c; *Critias* 107d; *Parmenides*, 142a, *Plato's Parmenides* (Trans. by R. E. Allen; Minneapolis: University of Minnesota Press, 1983); see Thomas Billings, *The Platonism of Philo Judaeus* (New York: Garland Publishing, 1979), pp. 17-18.

[13] For examples, see Paul S. Fiddes, *The Creative Suffering of God* (Oxford: Clarendon Press, 1988), pp. 53-54, referring to Thomas Aquinas, *Summa Theologica*, 1a.13.7; and John Sanders, *The God Who Risks: A Theology of Providence* (Downers Grove: Inter-Varsity Press, 1998), p.p. 150-151, referring to Augustine, *The City of God*, 22.2; also compare 9.5; and *On the Trinity*, 1.1.2.

[14] See especially book Alpha of *The Metaphysics*; references are to the Penguin Classics edition, translated by Hugh Lawson-Tancred (New York: Penguin Books, 1998).

[15] *The Metaphysics*, Book Lambda; and *Physics*, 8.5.

[16] *Metaphysics*, Lambda, 7h.

[17] *Metaphysics*, Lambda, 9a.

[18] *Metaphysics*, Lambda, 9c.

[19] *Metaphysics*, Lambda, 9c.

[20] Josephus, *Antiquities of the Jews*, 18.257-260; Eusebius, *Ecclesiastical History*, 2.4-5, 2.17; Philo, *On the Embassy to Gaius*.

[21] Billings, p. 3.

[22] *Ecclesiastical History*, 2.17. Also see Billings, pp. 1-6 on the Christianization of Philo.

[23] David T. Runia, *Philo and the Church Fathers* (Leiden: E. J. Brill, 1995),

NOTES

pp. 117, 191.

[24] Runia, *Philo and the Church Fathers*, p. 193.

[25] *Moses*, 1.21-48.

[26] *On Creation*, 15-20.

[27] *On Creation*, 20.

[28] *Allegorical Interpretation*, 1.51; 2.1-2; *Sacrifice of Abel and Cain*, 95-96; *On Dreams*, 1.231-236; to sample only a few.

[29] David T. Runia, *Philo in Early Christian Literature* (Minneapolis: Fortress Press, 1993), p. 338.

[30] *On the Changeableness of God*, 22; this quotation is from the translation of C. D. Yonge, *The Works of Philo* (Peabody, MA: Hendrickson, 1993).

[31] *On the Changeableness of God*, 53-55.

[32] *On the Changeableness of God*, 110.

[33] *On the Changeableness of God*, 53.

[34] *On the Changeableness of God*, 53.

[35] *On the Changeableness of God*, 63.

[36] *Stromateis [The Miscellanies]*, 1.7; 7.2.

[37] *Stromateis [The Miscellanies]*, 5.11.

[38] Runia, (1993), p. 133; (1995), p. 191. Clement mentions Philo by name 4 times.

[39] *Stromateis [The Miscellanies]*, 2.2.

[40] *Stromateis [The Miscellanies]*, 2.16.

[41] *Stromateis [The Miscellanies]*, 5.11; emphasis mine.

[42] *Stromateis [The Miscellanies]*, 5.12.

[43] *Stromateis [The Miscellanies]*, 2.16; 5.11.

[44] *Stromateis [The Miscellanies]*, 2.16; 4.23; 4.24; 5.11; 6.9; 7.3.

[45] *Stromateis [The Miscellanies]*, 5.12.

[46] *Paedagogus [The Instructor]*, 1.8.

[47] *Stromateis [The Miscellanies]*, 4.24; 5.11; 5.12; 7.2.

[48] *Stromateis [The Miscellanies]*, 6.9; also see 7.3.

[49] *Paedagogus*, 1.2.

[50] *Paedagogus*, 1.2.

[51] *Stromateis [The Miscellanies]*, 6.9.

[52] From Tertullian's complaint, "I am sorry from my heart that Plato has been

the caterer to all these heretics." Found in chapter 23, *A Treatise on the Soul*, *The Ante-Nicene Fathers*, vol. 3 (Grand Rapids: Eerdmans, 1951).

[53] Chapter 9; quotation from *The Ante-Nicene Fathers*, vol. 3, pp. 247f.

[54] *Prescription Against Heretics*, Chapter 7.

[55] *On the Flesh of Christ*, Chapter 5; for the translation of this difficult passage I have used Hans von Campenhausen, *The Fathers of the Latin Church* (Peabody, MA: Hendrickson, 1998), p. 23.

[56] *On the Flesh of Christ*; this paragraph is a synopsis of the argument developed in Chapter 5.

[57] Even though the following arguments are not systematically developed in any one location, they are each addressed to the same sets of questions scattered throughout a variety of Tertullian's writings.

[58] These observations are developed in *Against Marcion*, 2.16.

[59] *Against Marcion*, 2.16.

[60] See Joseph Hallman, *The Descent of God: Divine Suffering in History and Theology* (Minneapolis: Fortress Press, 1991), p. 54.

[61] This argument is developed in *On the Flesh of Christ*, Chapter 3.

[62] *Against Marcion*, 2.16.

[63] *Against Marcion*, 2.27.

[64] See von Campenhausen, p. 35.

[65] Especially as expressed in his work *Against Praxeas*, written during his later Montanist period! It is possible that Tertullian may have modified his earlier views on divine emotions in this work. However, given the apologetic and rhetorical purposes of the work, it is difficult to assess how he might has answered such questions.

[66] For a good discussion of these issues see Christopher Stead, *Philosophy in Christian Antiquity* (Cambridge: University Press, 1994), especially Part II, "The Use of Philosophy in Christian Theology."

[67] English reprint (Grand Rapids: Baker Books, 1978), p. 58.

CHAPTER 2

[1] *The Instructor*, 1.8, (*The Ante-Nicene Fathers*, vol. 2, Grand Rapids, 1951).

[2] *Against Celsus*, 4.72, (*The Ante-Nicene Fathers*, vol. 4, Grand Rapids, Eerdmans, 1951).

[3] All references are to *The Ante-Nicene Fathers*, vol. 7, (Grand Rapids, Eerdmans, 1951).

NOTES

[4] *On the Anger of God*, 5.

[5] *On the Anger of God*, 5.

[6] See the discussions in Terence Fretheim, *The Suffering of God* (Philadelphia: Fortress Press, 1984), pp. 65-67; Fiddes, *The Creative Suffering of God*, p. 24.

[7] Exodus 34:6; Numbers 14:18; Nehemiah 9:17; Psalms 86:15; 103:8; 145:8; Joel 2:13; Jonah 4:2; Nahum 1:3.

[8] Also Ezra 9:8; Psalm 85:3.

[9] *On the Anger of God*, 15.

[10] Ibid., 18.

[11] Quoted by Carol Tarvis, *Anger: The Misunderstood Emotion* (New York: Simon & Schuster, 1982), p. 251.

[12] There is an extensive body of literature dealing with metaphor and religious language. See Sallie McFague, *Metaphorical Theology: Models of God in Religious Language* (Philadelphia: Fortress Press, 1982); Jules Moreau, *Language and Religious Language* (Philadelphia: Westminster Press, 1961); David Tracy, *The Analogical Imagination: Christian Theology and the Culture of Pluralism*, (New York: Crossroad, 1981). On the importance of Biblical anthropomorphisms in the discussion of God's passibility, see T. E. Pollard, "The Impassibility of God," *The Scottish Journal of Theology*, bol. 8, 1955, pp. 353-364; Gerald Wondra, "The Pathos of God," *The Reformed Review*, vol. 18, 1964, pp. 28-35; Kenneth J. Woollcombe, "The Pain of God," *The Scottish Journal of Theology*, vol. 20, 1967, pp. 129-148; D. J. Clines, "Yahweh and the God of Christian Theology," *Theology*, September, 1980, pp. 323-330; Alan Torrance, "Does God Suffer? Incarnation and Impassiblity," in *Christ in Our Place*, (eds. Trevor Hart and Daniel Thimell, Exeter: The Paternoster Press, 1989), pp. 345-368.

[13] Literary critics describe "controlling metaphors" that must be taken as primary.

[14] *On the Anger of God*, 21.

[15] *On the Anger of God*, 21.

[16] *On the Anger of God*, 17.

[17] *On the Anger of God*, 22; emphasis mine.

CHAPTER 3

[1] See chapter one.

[2] *Nicomachean Ethics* (The Loeb Classical Library, Harvard: University Press, 1926), 8.11.3.

[3] *Eudemian Ethics* (The Loeb Classical Library, Harvard: University Press,

1935), 7.3.4; 7.4.5.

[4] *Eudemian Ethics*, 7.12.15-16.

[5] 2.380a-381d.

[6] In the New Testament, see James 2:23 for a similar statement.

[7] Abraham Heschel, *The Prophets*, 2 vols. (New York: HarperCollins, 1962), vol. 2, p. 39.

[8] *Against Heresies*, 4.37.6-7, (*The Ante-Nicene Fathers*, vol. 1, Grand Rapids: Eerdmans, 1956).

[9] *Against Marcion*, 2.6.

[10] *Against Heresies*, 4.37-41.

[11] *Against Marcion*, 2.5-10.

[12] *Miscellanies*, 2.15-16; 4.24-25; 7.7-8.

[13] *On First Principles*, 2.9.2; and the entirety of book 3 (*The Ante-Nicene Fathers*, vol. 4 Grand Rapids: Eerdmans, 1956).

[14] *The City of God*, 5.9; 22.30; *On the Spirit and the Letter*, 52-60 (*Nicene and Post-Nicene Fathers*, vols. 2 & 5, Grand Rapids: Eerdmans, 1956); *On Free Choice of the Will*, 1.12, 14, 16; 2.1, 18; especially 3.1-3, 16-18 (trans by Thomas Williams, [Indianapolis: Hackett Publication Company, 1993]); even granting that this was an early work, some of which Augustine retracted later in life, the reader will see that his fundamental outlook on free will remained essentially the same.

[15] *Against Marcion*, 2.5.

[16] Various forms of these doctrines, espoused by both Martin Luther and John Calvin, as well as other leaders of the 15th—16th Protestant Reformation, maintain that the human disinterest in God is so profound that only the Savior's eternal predetermination of who will be saved prevents all from being lost.

[17] *On the Spirit and the Letter*, 60.

[18] Heschel, *The Prophets*, vol. 2, p. 38.

[19] Also see his works, *God in Search of Man: A Philosophy of Judaism* (New York: Farrar, Strauss and Giroux, 1955); *Man is Not Alone: A Philosophy of Religion* (New York: Octagon Books, 1972).

[20] Heschel, *The Prophets*, vol. 2, pp. 3-4.

[21] See Lester Kuyper, "The Suffering and the Repentance of God," *Scottish Journal of Theology*. vo. 22, 1969, pp. 257-277; H. Van Dyke Parunak, "A Semantic Survey of NHM," *Biblica*. vol. 56, 1975, pp. 512-532; Terence Fretheim, "The Repentance of God: A Study of Jeremiah 18:7-10," *Hebrew Annual Review*, vol. 11, 1987, pp. 81-92; "The Repentance of God: A Key to Evaluating Old Testament God-Talk," *Horizons in Biblical Theology*. vol. 10, 1988, pp. 47-70; and the most

exhaustive, thorough survey I have found in Francis I. Andersen and David Noel Freedman, *Amos: A New Translation with Introduction and Commentary* (New York: Doubleday, 1989), "Excurses: When God Repents," pp. 638-679.

[22] *On the Unchangeableness of God*, 63.

[23] Also see Judges 2:18; II Samuel 24:16; I Chronicles 21:15; Psalms 135:14; Hosea 11:8; Jeremiah 42:10.

[24] Also see Psalms 90:13; 106:44-45; Isaiah 57:6; Jeremiah 26:3, 13, 19; Joel 2:13-14; Jonah 3:9-10; 4:2.

[25] Such as Numbers 23:19; I Samuel 15:29; Psalm 110:4; Jeremiah 4:28; 15:6; 20:16; Ezekiel 24:14; Hosea 13:14; Zechariah 8:14.

[26] Such as God's decision not to withdraw the kingship from David as it had been taken from Saul (I Samuel 15:29); see Terence Fretheim, "Divine Foreknowledge, Divine Constancy, and the Rejection of Saul's Kingship," *Catholic Biblical Quarterly*. vol. 47, 1985, pp. 595-602; a commitment never to abandon Judah's king (Psalm 110:4); or warnings that it is too late for Israel to avoid her punishment by Babylon (Jeremiah 4:28; 15:6).

[27] God always keeps a promise, whether to reward or to punish (Numbers 23:19; Jeremiah 20:16; Ezekiel 24:14; Hosea 13:14; Zechariah 8:14).

[28] See especially Terence Fretheim, *The Suffering of God: An Old Testament Perspective* (Philadelphia: Fortress, 1984), pp. 45-59.

[29] Isaiah 47:12; Jeremiah 26:2-3; 36:3, 7; 51:8; Ezekiel 12:1-3.

[30] Fiddes, *The Creative Suffering of God*, p. 220.

[31] There is a long standing debate over which type of knowledge of the future God has, but the details of that discussion need not detain us here.

[32] For further examples, see Terence Fretheim, "Suffering God and Sovereign God in Exodus: A Collision of Images," *Horizons in Biblical Theology*, vol. 11, 1989, pp. 31-55.

[33] Marcel Sarot, "Omnipotence and Self-limitation," in *Christian Faith and Philosophical Theology: Essays in Honour of Vincent Brümmer* (Dampen: Pharos Publishing, 1992), pp. 172-185.

[34] Emil Brunner, *The Christian Doctrine of Creation and Redemption*, (Philadelphia: Westminster Press, 1952), pp. 172-173; Fretheim, *The Suffering of God*, p. 58.

[35] Fiddes, *The Creative Suffering of God*, p. 24.

CHAPTER 4

[1] *Othello*, Act 2, scene 1, line 292; Act 3, scene 3, line 170.

² *Romantic Jealousy: Understanding and Conquering the Shadow of Love* (New York: St. Martin's Press, 1992).

³ The Septuagint (often designated as the LXX) is a Greek translation of the Hebrew Old Testament (begun in the 3rd century B.C.) that allows us to compare which Greek words were typically selected as synonyms for various Hebrew words.

⁴ David Buss, *The Dangerous Passion: Why Jealousy is as Necessary as Love and Sex* (New York: The Free Press, 2000), pp. 27-28, 220-221; Gordon Clanton, "Frontiers of Jealousy Research," *Jealousy*, edited by Gordon Clanton and Lynn Smith (New York, University Press of America, 1998, 3rd ed.), p. 242; Pines, *Romantic Jealousy*, p. 3.

⁵ For the distinction between rivals and trespassers in our appraisal of jealousy see, Kingsley Davis, "Jealousy and Sexual Property," *Jealousy*, pp. 129-131.

⁶ Gregory White and Paul Mullen, *Jealousy: Theory, Research, and Clinical Strategies*, (New York: The Guilford Press, 1989), pp. 2, 265; Clanton, "Jealousy in American Culture, 1945-1985," *Jealousy*, pp. 260-261.

⁷ For this historical survey of the literature see appendices I, II, and IV by Clanton, "Frontiers of Jealousy Research", "Jealousy in American Culture" and "A Sociology of Jealousy," in *Jealousy*; many of the essays found in this collection aptly illustrate the different perspectives under discussion; also see, Pines, *Romantic Jealousy*, pp. 135-140.

⁸ *The Dangerous Passion*, p. 221.

⁹ See Chris Downing, "Jealousy: A Depth-psychological Perspective," *Jealousy*, pp. 72-79; Pines, *Romantic Jealousy*, pp. 52-55; White, *Jealousy*, pp. 76-83; for some first-hand reading see, Sigmund Freud, *The Interpretation of Dreams*, The Complete Psychological Works of Sigmund Freud, vol. 4 (London: The Hogarth Press, 1953), pp. 262-265.

¹⁰ See White, *Jealousy*, p. 266 for some examples of how Freud's theories fail to find support in current research.

¹¹ (New York: Howell, Soskin Publishers), pp. 9-10, 260.

¹² p. 262.

¹³ Margaret Mead, "Jealousy: Primitive and Civilised," *Jealousy*, pp. 116, 120; reprinted from *Woman's Coming of Age*, edited by Samuel D. Schmalhausen and V. F. Calverton (New York, Horace Liveright, Inc., 1931).

¹⁴ For the details of this fascinating story see the kind but damning works of anthropologist Derek Freeman, *Margaret Mead and Samoa: The Making and Unmaking of an Anthropological Myth*, (Cambridge, Harvard University Press, 1983); and *The Fateful Hoaxing of Margaret Mead: A Historical Analysis of Her*

NOTES

Samoan Research (Boulder, Westview Press, 1999); the quote is from p. 1; also see Buss, *The Dangerous Emotion*, pp. 31, 72; Clanton, *Jealousy*, pp. 126-127.

[15] See White, *Jealousy*, pp. 262-263 for a discussion of the differences among normal, pathological and symptomatic jealousies.

[16] Pines, *Romantic Jealousy*, pp. 49-51.

[17] See pp. 265-275.

[18] John 3:16 (that famous quote from the endzone), "God loves the world so much that the one and only Son was given so that whoever believes in him will not be lost but will have eternal life."

[19] 1 Timothy 2:4, "God our Savior...wants all people to be saved and to come to a knowledge of the truth."

[20] Clanton, "Jealousy in American Culture, 1945-1985," *Jealousy*, pp. 272-275.

[21] White, *Jealousy*, pp. 256-257.

[22] Buss, *The Dangerous Emotion*, pp. 87-93; Clanton, "Frontiers of Jealousy Research," pp. 248-249; "Developmental Correlates of Jealousy," p. 288; "A Sociology of Jealousy," pp. 300-303, 309, all in *Jealousy*; Pines, *Romantic Jealousy*, pp. 39-40; White, *Jealousy*, pp. 104-127, 266.

[23] See Pines' discussion of pathological tolerance and psychological scotoma (ie., blindness) in *Romantic Jealousy*, pp. 49-50.

[24] *Homilies on Ezekiel*, 6.6; English versions of the relevant paragraph are found in McLelland, *God the Anonymous*, p. 123; Hans Urs von Balthasar, *Origen: Spirit and Fire, A Thematic Anthology of His Writings* (Washington, D.C.: Catholic University of America Press), p. 122, paragraph 269, although here the source is not clearly identified; for the complete homily in Latin and French see, Marcel Borret, *Homélies sur Ézéchiel: Texte Latin, Introduction, Traduction et Notes*, (Paris: Cerf), pp. 227-231.

CHAPTER 5

[1] G. K. Chesterton referred to "'The Hound of Heaven' the greatest religious poem of modern times"; see *The Hound of Heaven and Other Poems*, (Boston, International Pocket Library, 1936), p. 5. Its author, Francis Thompson (1859-1907), spent much of his life a homeless, opium addict sleeping in the sewers of Victorian London. The poem, composed after his conversion to Christianity, reflects his understanding of God's grace. This is from the conclusion of stanza 3:

> Nigh and nigh draws the chase,
> With unperturbèd pace,

> Deliberate speed, majestic instancy;
> And past those noisèd Feet
> A voice comes yet more fleet –
> 'Lo! naught contents thee, who content'st not Me.'

[2] Also see Isaiah 7:13 and Malachi 2:17.

[3] Karen H. Jobes and Moisés Silva, *Invitation to the Septuagint* (Grand Rapids, Baker Academic, 2000), p. 19.

[4] In Jeremiah 15:6, God is not "weary of changing his mind" but "will no longer bear their sins." In Isaiah 1:14, "I am weary of bearing your sins" becomes "I will no longer remit your sins." In Isaiah 7:13, "Will you also weary God's patience?" becomes "How is it that you cause strife for the Lord?" Isaiah 43:24, "You have wearied me with your offenses" becomes "You stood before me in your sins and your offenses." Malachi 2:17, "You have wearied me with your words" becomes "You have provoked God with your words."

[5] "God gives strength to the weary / and increases the power of the weak. / Even youths grow tired and weary, / and young men stumble and fall . . ."

[6] See Alan E. Bernstein, *The Formation of Hell: Death and Retribution in the Ancient and Early Christian Worlds* (Ithaca: Cornell University Press, 1993), especially pp. 1-83; also "A Brief History of Hell" in Charles Seymour, *A Theodicy of Hell* (Dordrecht/Boston/London: Kluwer Academic Publishers, 2000), pp. 15-35.

[7] *Phaedo* 113e.

[8] See Psalm 69:28; Daniel 10:21; 12:1.

[9] Jonathan L. Kvanvig, *The Problem of Hell* (Oxford: University Press, 1993), p. 148.

[10] See D. P. Walker, *The Decline of Hell: Seventeenth-Century Discussions of Eternal Torment*, (London, Routledge & Kegan Paul, 1964); Geoffrey Rowell, *Hell and the Victorians: A study of the nineteenth-century theological controversies concerning eternal punishment and the future life* (Oxford: Clarendon Press, 1974).

[11] *The Problem of Hell*, p. 17.

[12] *The Problem of Hell*, p. 153.

[13] Chaos theory maintains that every natural event, no matter how seemingly random, is intertwined with every other event. So that hurricanes in the northern hemisphere may trace their origins back to the fluttering of butterfly wings in the southern hemisphere.

[14] The Apostle's Creed is an early ecumenical Christian confession developed between the third to sixth centuries A.D.:

I believe in God, the Father almighty,
> creator of heaven and earth.

I believe in Jesus Christ, his only Son, our Lord,
> who was conceived by the Holy Spirit
> and born of the virgin Mary.
> He suffered under Pontius Pilate,
> was crucified, died, and was buried;
> he descended to hell.
> The third day he rose again from the dead.
> He ascended to heaven
> and is seated at the right hand of God the Father almighty.
> From there he will come to judge the living and the dead.

I believe in the Holy Spirit,
> the holy catholic church,
> the communion of saints,
> the forgiveness of sins,
> the resurrection of the body,

and the life everlasting. Amen.

[15] *The Prophets*, vol. 1, p.82.

CHAPTER 6

[1] *Shame: The Exposed Self* (New York: The Free Press, 1995), p. 127.

[2] Obviously, in these examples I am simplifying the nature of emotional interaction for the sake of making a point. I realize that few relationships are this straightforward. It is always possible for us to offer a contrary response to another's emotional overtures.

[3] See Paul Gilbert and Bernice Andrews (eds.), *Shame: Interpersonal Behavior, Pschopathology, and Culture* (Oxford: Oxford University Press, 1998), p. 17.

[4] *The Myserious Flame: Conscious Minds in a Material World*, (New York, Basic Books, 1999).

[5] (New York, Grosset/Putnam's Sons, 1994); also *The Feeling of What Happens: Body and Emotion in the Making of Consciousness* (New York: Harcourt Brace & Co., 1999). Also compare such work as Daniel Goleman, *Emotional Intelligence: Why It Can Matter More than IQ*, (New York, Bantam Books, 1995).

[6] Carl Goldberg, *Understanding Shame* (London: Jason Aronson Inc., 1991), pp. 41-42; Gilbert and Andrews, *Shame*, p. 27.

[7] Goldberg, *Understanding Shame*, p. 279; Lewis, *Shame*, pp. 143-149.

[8] This story and the following discussion is based upon V. S. Ramachandran

and Sandra Blakeslee, *Phantoms in the Brain: Probing the Mysteries of the Human Mind* (New York: William Morrow & Co., 1998), pp. 174-198.

[9] Also see Russell Shorto, *Saints and Madmen: Psychiatry Opens Its Doors to Religion* (New York, Henry Holt & Co., 1999), pp. 188-196.

[10] *Saints and Madmen*, pp. 159-196, 230-236; also see Ralph W. Hook, "The Construction and Preliminary Validation of a Measure of Reported Mystical Experience," *Journal for the Scientific Study of Religion*. volume 14, 1975, pp. 29-41; Edward M. Podvoll, "Psychosis and the Mystic Path," *Psychoanalytic Review*, volume 66, 179-80, pp. 571-590; Peter Buckley, "Mystical Experience and Schizophrenia," *Schizophrenea Bulletin*. volume 7, 1981, pp. 516-521; Kenneth Stifler, Joanne Greer, William Sneck and Robert Dovenmuehle, "An Empirical Investigation of the Discriminability of Reported Mystical Experiences Among Religious Contemplative, Psychotic Inpatients, and Normal Adults," *Journal for the Scientific Study of Religion*. volume 32, 1993, 366-372; Jeffrey S. Levin, David B. Larson and Christina M. Puchalski, "Religion and Spirituality in Medicine: Research and Education," *Journal of the American Medical Association*. vol. 278, September 3, 1997, pp. 792-793.

[11] *Phantoms in the Brain*, pp. 179, 188.

[12] Even though some would argue with calling them "emotions," I will use this term because guilt and shame are both things that we "feel."

[13] Gerhart Piers and Milton Singer, *Shame and Guilt: A Psychoanalytic and a Cultural Study*, (New York, W. W. Norton & Co., 1971); Carl Schneider, *Shame, Exposure, and Privacy* (Boston: Beacon Press, 1977); Agnes Heller, *The Power of Shame: A Rational Perspective* (London: Routledge & Kegan Paul, 1985); Susan Miller, *The Shame Experience* (London: The Analytic Press, 1985); Merle Fossum and Marilyn Mason, *Facing Shame: Families in Recovery* (New York: W. W. Norton & Co., 1986); Gershen Kaufman, *The Psychology of Shame: Theory and Treatment of Shame-Based Syndromes* (New York: Springer Publishing Co., 1989); Goldberg, *Understanding Shame*; Lewis, *Shame: The Exposed Self*; Andrew Morrison, *The Culture of Shame* (New York: Ballantine Books, 1996); Gilbert and Andrews, *Shame: Interpersonal Behavior*.

[14] Fossum and Mason, *Facing Shame*, p. vii.

[15] Many authors do speak of guilt and shame as if they are easily isolated. For the more nuanced position taken here see, Heller, *The Power of Shame*, pp. 2-13; Miller, *The Shame Experience*, pp. 46-49, 141-142; Kaufman, *The Psychology of Shame*, pp. 6-7, 26.

[16] Schneider, *Shame, Exposure and Privacy*, does an admirable job of demonstrating that all shame is not intrinsically unhealthy as many would have us believe; in fact, it is an essential mark of a human being.

NOTES

[17] For some suggestions on therapeutic method, see Goldberg, *Understanding Shame*, pp. 274-281; Morrison, *The Culture of Shame*, pp. 108-132.

[18] See Heller, *The Power of Shame*, pp. 9-11.

[19] E. Allison Peers (ed. and trans.), *The Life of Teresa of Jesus: The Autobiography of St. Teresa of Avila* (New York: Image Books, 1960), p. 40.

[20] Evelyn Underhill, *Mysticism: The Nature and Development of Spiritual Consciousness* (Oxford: Oneworld Publications, 1993, reprint), p. 274.

[21] E. Allison Peers (ed. and trans.), *Interior Castle* (New York: Image Books, 1961), pp. 139-140.

[22] To my knowledge, Teresa never suggests that depression *per se* is a spiritual problem or the result of demonic powers. She seems quite open to its being a human condition that may come and go.

[23] Peers, *The Life of Teresa of Jesus*, pp. 235-236.

[24] Peers, *Interior Castle*, p. 141.

[25] Peers, *Interior Castle*, p. 142.

[26] Peers, *The Life of Teresa of Jesus*, p. 237.

[27] Peers, *Interior Castle*, p. 145.

[28] Peers, *Interior Castle*, p. 144.

[29] Peers, *Interior Castle*, p. 140.

[30] *Being and Nothingness* (Trans. H. E. Barnes; New York: Philosophical Library, 1956), pp. 221-222; quoted in Morrison, *The Culture of Shame*, p. 6.

CHAPTER 7

[1] von Campenhausen, *The Fathers of the Church*, 1.81.

[2] Quoted in von Campenhausen, p. 80.

[3] Matthew 19:21; see Athanasius, *The Life of Antony* (The Classics of Western Spirituality, New York: Paulist Press, 1980), 2.

[4] *The Life of Antony*, 67.

[5] *The Life of Antony*, 20.

[6] *St. Athanasius on the Incarnation: The Treatise "De Incarnatione Verbi Dei"* (Crestwood, New York: St. Valdimir's Orthodox Theological Seminary, 1953), 54.

[7] For the relevant references, see *St. Athanasius on the Incarnation*, p. 142, note 1.

[8] *Discourses Against the Arians*, 2.59

[9] William Fairweather, *Origen and Greek Patristic Thought* (Edinburgh: T. & T. Clark, 1901), p. 184.

[10] Fairweather, *Origen*, p. 184; although this is not to ignore the significant differences between the ways Origen and Athanasius each developed their notions of deification.

[11] See *Against Heresies*, 3.19.1.

[12] Athanasius, *Discourses Against the Arians* (Nicene and Post-Nicene Fathers of the Christian Church, second series, vol. 4; Grand Rapids, Eerdmans Publishing, 1991, reprint), 3.31, 32.

[13] For a discussion of this concept of the incarnation producing human receptivity to God's indwelling Spirit, see Khaled Anatolios, *Athanasius: The Coherence of His Thought* (London: Routledge, 1998), pp. 158-161, and notes 161-162 on pp. 239-240.

[14] *Discourses Against the Arians*, 3.34.

[15] *Letter to Epictetus* (Nicene and Post-Nicene Fathers of the Christian Church, second series, vol. 4, Grand Rapids, Eerdmans Publishing, 1991, reprint), 6.

[16] *Athanasius: The Coherence of His Thought*, p. 144.

[17] *St. Athanasius on the Incarnation*, 54.

[18] *Discourses Against the Arians*, 2.59.

[19] *Discourses Against the Arians*, 3.34.

[20] *Discourses Against the Arians*, 3.33.

[21] See *Athanasius: The Coherence of His Thought*, pp. 144-145.

[22] *The Prophets*, 2.267.

www.ingramcontent.com/pod-product-compliance
Lightning Source LLC
Chambersburg PA
CBHW062038220426
43662CB00010B/1550

FEELING LIKE GOD